Indian Women of the Western Morning

The Books of

JOHN UPTON TERRELL

Indian Women of the Western Morning—(WITH DONNA M. TERRELL)

Pueblos, Gods and Spaniards	Land Grab
Apache Chronicle	Bunkhouse Papers
American Indian Almanac	The Navajo
The Man Who Rediscovered America	La Salle
Traders of the Western Morning	The Six Turnings
Journey into Darkness	Black Robe
Zebulon Pike	Furs By Astor
Estevanico the Black	War for the Colorado River
Faint the Trumpet Sounds	Plume Rouge
Pueblo de los Corazones	Adam Cargo
Sunday Is the Day You Rest	The Little Dark Man

(Twelve works for young readers not listed)

John Upton Terrell & Donna M. Terrell

Indian Women of the Western Morning

Their Life in Early America

The Dial Press
New York
1974

To a good friend and a fine editor
William B. Decker

Manufactured in the United States of America

Design by Lynn Braswell

First printing

Library of Congress Cataloging in Publication Data

Terrell, John Upton, 1900–
Indian women of the western morning.

Bibliography: p.
1. Indians of North America—Women. I. Terrell,
Donna M., joint author. II. Title.
E98.W8T47   301.41'2'09701   74–10638
ISBN 0-8037-4351-3

In this book we have tried to portray American Indian women as they appeared, to tell something of their spiritual beliefs and their ways of life, at the beginning of recorded history—in the western morning.

J.U.T.
D.M.T.

Contents

Indian Women of the
Western Morning

1
Beginnings

*In the beginning God created
the Heaven and the Earth.*

The biblical story of *something* being created from *nothing* has
no equivalent in the origin myths of Indians.

Without exception, the many systems of Indian mythology, while varying greatly in minor details, relate that an orderly universe existed *from the beginning of time.* And ever
since the mysterious advent of this cosmos there were contin-
ual changes—metamorphosis in all things, both animate and
inanimate—brought about by inexplicable but obviously in-
superable forces of nature.

No less subject to these magical transitions than any other
natural entity, Indians eventually reached the present surface
world after imprisonment for immeasurable ages in various

older regions. Some of these older regions had been *below*, locked in eternal darkness, and some had been *above*, in the illimitable realms beyond the visible sky.

The concept that woman was made from man is not found in Indian religion. Indians accept and adhere to the doctrine that the female of their kind was created simultaneously with the male. For apparent reasons, each was endowed with peculiar qualities and sensibilities, neither was accorded supremacy, and each was made dependent upon the other for existence.

How could it be otherwise? For all living things—every plant, every animal, every fish and fowl, even the smallest insect—come into being only after completion of the cycle that makes their respective lives possible.

To an Indian it would be the height of irrationality to assert that woman was made from the rib bone of a man. The natural processes, unceasing in their functioning, negate the allegation that one sex could have been created without the other.

Yet, despite this conceptual practicality, no sacred narratives, no allegorical expressions, are more imaginative, more fabulous, more permeated by mysticism, than those of the Indians. Two examples that vividly illustrate this fact are the origin myths of the Tewa Pueblos and the Navajo, two peoples whose traditional cultures embraced sharp contrasts.*

---

* The Tewa are a dialectical group of the Tanoan linguistic family (the other branches being the Tiwa, Jemez, and Piro), and are among the oldest inhabitants of the American Southwest. At the beginning of the historical period they dwelt in at least thirty pueblos. Six of these ancient towns are still occupied by them, namely, Nambe, Pojoaque, San Ildefónso, Santa Clara, Tesuque, and San Juan, all in the general Santa Fe region. The Athapascan linguistic family, to which the Navajo belong, was at one time the largest and most widely distributed linguistic family in North America, extending from the Arctic to northern Mexico and from the Pacific

In the beginning the Tewa lived in an underworld called Sipofene that lay beneath a large lake, far to the north of their southwestern homeland. Alfonso Ortiz, a social anthropologist born in San Juan Pueblo, writes: *

The world under the lake was like this one, but it was dark. Supernaturals, men, and animals lived together at this time, and death was unknown. Among the supernaturals were the first mothers of all the Tewa, known as *Blue Corn Woman, near to summer,* or the Summer Mother, and *White Corn Maiden, near to ice,* the Winter Mother.

These mothers asked one of the men present to go forth and explore the way by which the people might leave the lake.

The man went, making four trips, one in each direction, but saw nothing but "mist and haze."

He reported that the world above was "ochu" (green and unripe).

Sent out again, he

came upon an open place and saw all the *tsiwi* [predatory mammals and carrion-eating birds] gathered there. . . . On seeing the man these animals rushed him, knocked him down, and scratched him badly. Then they spoke, telling him: "Get up! We are your friends." His wounds vanished immediately. The animals gave him a bow and arrows and a quiver, dressed him in buckskin, painted his face black, and tied the feathers of the carrion-eaters on his hair. Finally they told him: "You have been accepted. These things

---

Coast to the mouth of the Rio Grande. The Navajo are believed to have migrated slowly, over a long period, from northern and western Canada to New Mexico and Arizona in relatively late prehistoric times, perhaps no earlier than the eighth century A.D.

* *The Tewa World.*

we have given you are what you shall use henceforth. Now you are ready to go."

When he returned to the people below, the first explorer of the Above went as "Mountain Lion, or Hunt Chief. This is how the first *Made* person came into being."

Hunt Chief appointed a Summer Chief and a Winter Chief by handing each an ear of white corn. They became the next Made persons, and they were to lead the people to the Above. Six pairs of brothers called *Towa é* were sent out. Each pair was a different color. The blue, yellow, red, and white pairs reported seeing mountains in each of the cardinal directions. The dark pair saw a large star in the eastern sky. The all-colored pair saw a rainbow.

The people started. Summer Chief led the way, but found the surface soft mud. When Winter Chief stepped on it the ground hardened. And the people began to emerge from the dark underworld. But many became ill, and all returned below, where the original corn mothers and other supernaturals had remained. Summer Chief and Winter Chief agreed that the people were not yet complete, and that "something else was needed."

Fear of ghosts, witchcraft, and sorcery was intense in all primitive Indians. Each tribe had its own legend telling how these frightening practices were discovered. The Tewa myth, according to Ortiz, relates that when the people returned to their home beneath the lake because so many were ill,

Hunt Chief opened up Summer Chief's corn mother. He discovered that the hollow core was filled with pebbles, ashes, and cactus spines. The Hunt Chief replaced these with seeds and declared that one among the people . . . was a witch, for the items discovered in the corn mother were recognized as items of witchcraft. This, then, marked the beginning of witchcraft and other forms of evil. In order to combat these and to make the people well, the *Ke* (medicine man) was created as the fourth *Made* person.

After being obliged to return to the underworld three times to resolve serious problems in their characters and cultural structure, the Tewa felt they were complete, and they emerged and moved southward along the Rio Grande. Standing watch on the four mountains of the directions were the Towa é, the four pairs of blue, yellow, red, and white brothers.

Women not only hold high rank among Indian supernaturals, but in the pantheons of some Indian peoples they possess spiritual powers commensurable with those of some male gods. Those who offer pleas and prayers to the Sky Father also pay obeisance to the Earth Mother, fearing to offend her. And many Indians think of the Morning Star as the male star and the Evening Star as the female star; the Sun is male and the Moon is female.

In the Navajo genesis, both men and women evolved through four underworlds before reaching the earth's surface. These nether regions and the sun world are portrayed as superimposed hemispheres, the skies of which are supported by deities.

In the first Navajo underworld there were four clouds, which embodied the prototypes of males and females. First Man was created when two of the clouds met in the east, and First Woman was created when the two other clouds met in the west. Although First Man and First Woman lived together, they did not produce mankind, for they were merely prototypes, and not in themselves human beings. But in this darkness it was predestined that human beings should be, for First Man and First Woman planned their creation, and, with the cooperation of many other types of beings— that is, animate natural entities among whom they dwelt— they also planned all other developments for the surface world on which human beings eventually would live.

The emergence of human beings was slow and difficult. In the second underworld the Navajo prototypes fought with bird beings before moving up to the third underworld. There they encountered Holy People, and other kinds of beings. And it was in the third underworld that a miraculous event took place. There the emerging people found the prototype of Changing Woman, who represented fertility and life, its regeneration and recession with the seasons.

But the third underworld was not without misfortunes. The sexes were temporarily separated, with the result that monster beings were born. Water Monster produced a flood that drove all other beings upward to the fourth un- derworld.* After a hard struggle, the sexes were reunited, but Monster Beings continued to make the fourth un- derworld a fearful place, and at last First Man and First Woman led everyone up to the fifth world, the surface.

All the prototypes of animate and inanimate objects— which were both male and female, even the mountains and the rivers and other geographical phenomena—were also brought up to the fifth world, and there assumed the forms in which they would forever remain. And in accordance with the cosmic plan formulated in the lower worlds, the sun, the moon and the stars took the places assigned to them, and so

---

* A story of a great flood is contained in many Indian creation fables.

night and day and spring and summer and fall and winter were established.

The Holy People went to live on four sacred mountains that mark, one in each direction, the boundaries of Dinetah, the land of the Navajo.*

And ever since, when the Holy People have wished to take a journey, they have traveled on sunbeams, rainbows, and lightning. And Changing Woman, who is blessed with eternal youth and incomparable beauty, dwells in a great house beside the western sea.

While the mythological accounts of numerous Indian peoples are similar to the Tewa and Navajo creation stories in that they speak of ascent from one or more underworlds, those of other groups tell of descent from upperworlds.

The origin myths of many tribes of the immense Siouan linguistic family relate that they floated down to the present surface earth after an extensive period during which they passed through three sky worlds that lay one above another.

The Iroquois, according to their mythology, were originally Sky People, dwelling on a disc far above the earth. Their origin myth is unique in the respect that it recounts how one pregnant woman was the first to descend from the place of creation in the sky.

Recounts Ruth M. Underhill: †

---

* The four mountains are known today as Big Sheep Peak in the La Plata Range on the north; Mount Taylor in New Mexico on the south; Humphreys Peak of the San Francisco Peaks in Arizona on the west; and Pelado Mountain in the Jemez Range on the east. Some Navajo singers maintain that the eastern sacred mountain is Sierra Blanca Peak in Colorado, thus the names of both mountains appear in Navajo legends.

† *Red Man's Religion.*

She fell toward an earth that was covered with water. The water birds saw her coming and spread their wings to float her down. Then they dived under water and brought up earth. . . . The Great Turtle, one of the earth's original inhabitants, offered his back to support the new land; and he has always been a spirit highly revered by the Iroquois. . . .

[The sky woman] bore a daughter. Later, the daughter bore a son, whether by Turtle or the North Wind the myths cannot agree. Here we have a culture hero who was half of the sky people and half, perhaps, of earth.*

Particularly interesting is the origin myth of the Osage, an important Siouan people, for it relates that a division of their tribe was indigenous to earth, dwelling there long before others descended from the sky to join them.

In a moving interpretation of Osage mythology, John Joseph Matthews, himself an Osage, writes: †

They were pure and clean and noble because they had just come from the stars—from among the stars, say the holy men . . . when they descended to earth, the Sacred One, they found her divided into land and water. . . .

The Little Old Men [wise men, storytellers] of today are sufficiently realistic to admit that the Sky People were befuddled when they first descended to earth, the Sacred One, but there is never a hint as to why they descended to the tragedy of long adjustment to earth and its disorder. Did Wah'Kon-Tah [Great Mystery Power] send them down in Jehovian anger, because they transgressed his laws? They have never intimated that there was an express reason for their descent.

* *Ibid.*

† *The Osages.*

They were quite modest before the mighty manifestations of the Great Mysteries, and meek before earth's anger and whims, and referred to themselves as the Little Ones.

They had been children, as well, up in the sky, children of

Grandfather the Sun, and as they say, noble and clean and shy and befuddled and inquisitive . . . but there was order in the descent to earth, since they were from the orderly sky. . . . They came to earth in three groups or divisions, but these did not constitute the whole tribe. There was one division indigenous to earth.

When the Children of the Middle Waters, who in their humility called themselves the Little Ones, came down from the stars, they floated down into a red oak tree, and as they alighted they loosened acorns which clattered down among the leaves. . . . They must have come down singly or in small groups. . . . They floated down from the sky with their legs outstretched to the tree tops, and their arms up like the wings of an alighting eagle, since it is this great bird's landing which they later imitated in their creation dances.

On earth, the children from the sky divided into three groups, each taking a name. They walked upon the Sacred One in order:

the People of the Water led, then came the People of the Land, and the People of the Sky last.

But it is not known by the modern Little Old Men when the three divisions, the People of the Water, the People of the Sky, and the People of the Land came upon the earthly village of the Isolated Earth People.

The origin myths of the Creeks present numerous variations, for they are a people of mixed ancestry who united and eventually formed a loose confederacy, the nucleus of which was a group of tribes called Muskogee. However, they held in common the belief that they once lived in the sky in spirit form, and after descending to earth became flesh and blood people.

In Creek theology the supreme supernatural was a rather vaguely defined being known as Esaugetu Emissee (Master of Breath), who dwelt in an upper realm of which the sky was the floor. Esaugetu Emissee, with the power to give and to take away the breath of life, may be identified with the Great Spirit and the Great Mystery recognized by other tribes.

David H. Corkran states: * "In religion the Creeks belong to the tradition of fire and water as manifestations of the great creator above."

An early traveler in the South, William Bartram,† reported that the Creeks paid "homage to the sun, moon, and planets as mediators or ministers of the Great Spirit."

Various types of ceremonies were held by the Creeks throughout the year, but the most important ritual was the Púskita, the Green Corn Dance (called by colonial observers *Boskitau*, or, more popularly, *Busk*), which lasted four days in small communities and as long as eight days in large towns. It was an occasion, so to speak, for beginning life anew, as the new corn appeared and ripened. It involved extinguishing old fires, discarding the ashes, and lighting new fires. The body was cleansed by ceremonial bathing, and the mind was purified by partaking of a powerful concoction to which the first British traders gave the name "black drink."

Wrote Bertram:

* *The Creek Frontier.*

† *Observations on the Creek and Cherokee Indians.*

12

When a town celebrates the busk, having previously provided themselves with new clothes, new pots, pans, and other household utensils and furniture, they collect all their worn-out clothes and other dispicable things, sweep and cleanse their houses, squares, and the whole town of their filth, which with all the remaining grain and other old provisions, they cast together into one common heap and consume it with fire. After having taken medicine [black drink], and fasted for three days, all the fire in the town is extinguished. During this fast they abstain from the gratification of every appetite and passion whatever. A general amnesty is proclaimed, all malefactors may return to their town, and they are absolved from their crimes, which are now forgotten, and they are restored to favor.

The black drink was made by boiling leaves of *Ilex cassine* in water. According to the Indian scholar Walter Hough,*

the action of the drink in strong infusion is purgative, vomitive, and diuretic. . . . the plant contains caffeine, the leaves yielding a beverage with stimulating qualities. . . . excessive indulgence produces nervous disturbance.

Excerpts from an account of the Busk by John Howard Payne,† prepared in the early nineteenth century, provide material regarding women's participation in the great ceremony. The people of a community, stated Payne, "made their year commence with the moon which had its first appearance about the time of Green Corn."

Seven ears of new corn were plucked from seven different fields belonging to seven different clans by a delegate as-

* *Bulletin 30*, Bureau of American Ethnology.

† *Cherokee Manuscripts*, quoted by Corkran, *op. cit.*

signed to the mission by religious leaders. In the late afternoon of the first day of the ceremony, which had been spent in feasting,

each woman was directed to repair to her house, extinguish all the old fire, throw out all the brands and ashes and cleanse her whole house, and all her household furniture. Men were also appointed to cleanse the council house and the sacred square in every part.

At dawn the following morning, according to Payne,

the priest appointed men to make new fire. . . . Immediately on the fire being kindled, the priest offered the sacrifice, that is, he took several kernels of corn from the seven ears . . . and threw them into the fire, together with a small piece of meat, praying etc. This being done the women and children might partake of the new fruits.

The women were ordered by the master of the ceremony to

take the new fire to their house, and feed it with sound wood of seven kinds of trees . . . and to keep it burning with those kinds of wood four days, not suffering it to go out.

. . . But women being in any kind of uncleanness could not work or warm by the new fire, nor partake of the green fruit; but used the old fruit and the old food out in the woods or in a tent for the purpose until the time of their separation was ended. Then they washed their flesh,—their clothes, their utensils, etc., and partook of the fruits of the new year and the benefits of the new fires.

. . . Before the women retired with the new fire, they were told when to return for the purpose of being purified with the water of purification. . . . It was made of the roots of a small kind of willow. These were pounded and put into two large pots, which were then filled with water. One of these was for the men, and one for the women and children. All drank of the water . . . and washed more or less with it and were then considered clean from the pollutions of the past year.

. . . At twelve o'clock on this day the priest appointed two singers for the men and two for the women, and selected two women to lead the female dance. . . . The women danced in a place by themselves, and the two men appointed to sing for them were seated on a bench near them. The men danced in the sacred square. . . . The dance of both parties continued until night. The men then repaired to a river and washed. They then returned and ate of old fruit having fasted all day, except as they drank of the water above mentioned or the black drink. . . . They then spent the night dancing. This part they continued thus four days. During this time they must not go to their houses, nor have any intercourse with their wives. Each day was spent in dancing, and drinking the purifying water and black drink, till near night when they repaired to the water, washed and returned and partook of food of old corn, and again spent the night in dancing. Thus they not only denied themselves of food during the day, but also of sleep during the night, for four nights successively.

On the morning after the fourth night of the fast and the fifth of the festival, the women brought the new corn etc. cooked and set down near the sacred square. The men then for the last time repaired to the water and washed. Being now considered clean from all impurities they partook of the new fruits and the feast closed.

The Creeks believed that the Master of Breath, who dwelt in their place of origin, the sky, had instructed the first of their people to reach the earth to perform the ceremonies of the Busk. The Great Master also had advised them that adherence to the new fire and purification rituals would entitle them to his care and protection in times of serious difficulties.

But whether an Indian people believes their place of origin to be an underworld or an upper world, or whether they believe their creation occurred through some other magic formula resulting from a blending of natural forces, there is nothing in any Indian mythology to suggest the principle that man preceded woman. However or from wherever they reached the surface earth on which they still dwell, then, man and woman reached it together.

Just as in the case of the biblical fables, science casts an impenetrable cloud over the imagery and fantasy of Indian origin myths. Indians reached North America from Siberia. They crossed the present Bering Strait when it was dry land.

That a land bridge (or bridges) between Asia and North America existed for a very long time during the Pleistocene Glacial Age has been indisputably proven by both zoological and geological evidence. The same animals lived in both regions. During the Ice Age sea levels were much lower than at present, because a large part of the world's water was locked in great glaciers. The water that made the glaciers came from the sea in the form of fog and clouds. It fell as snow. The glaciated regions were so intensely cold that annual summer melting was less than winter precipitation. The glaciers began to build up. Over enormous areas the icecap was a mile high, but in some localities it reached a height of nine thousand feet.

The Bering Strait is shallow. If the present water level fell only 125 feet, the strait would not exist. It would once more be a land bridge between the two continents. Moreover, it is only 56 miles in width, and this distance is broken by islands. The widest expanse of open sea is only 25 miles, and on a clear day people on one side can see the opposite coast.

A land bridge would have provided grass for grazing animals. And the people to be called Indians followed the animals, living both with them and on them. For these people were first hunters and second food gatherers.

Never was all of northern North America covered by ice at one time. Through countless millennia, as climatological metamorphoses occurred, glaciers advanced and retreated, reaching deep into the continent and withdrawing, scarring the earth and changing its contours. In their wakes they left warmth, and great lakes, and even deserts.

Important as far as the migrant from Asia is concerned is the geological knowledge that for long periods there were ice-free corridors through which both animals and men could have lived and passed. As an example, consider the last major glacial period of some twenty-five thousand years ago. Its center was in the vicinity of Hudson Bay. Far to the west there was considerably less ice, and there were ice-free corridors opening the way to the south. However, there were known to be what geologists call interstadials, periods when ice would not have confronted man with impassable barriers. And that man had reached the region of the United States several thousand years before the last major glaciation can no longer be questioned—scientists have recovered the evidence.

Man did not originate in the New World. He evolved from brute ancestry in the Old World and reached North America by way of the Bering Strait land bridge only, as Harold E. Driver states,*

after he had become modern physically and a member of the single species of modern man called *Homo sapiens,* wise man. Man's nearest animal relatives, the anthropoid apes, are all found in the

* *Indians of North America.*

Old World today: the chimpanzee and gorilla in Africa, the orang and gibbon in Southeast Asia and the neighboring continental islands. Man's next nearest animal relatives, the catarrhine monkeys, are likewise all confined to the Old World.

It is in the shifting of animals that much of the answer to the question of why people came to North America is to be found. When northern Europe was glaciated, as Carleton S. Coon * explains, the animals moved southward and eastward, reaching southern Europe and north central Asia, both of which were free of ice. The people depended upon these animals for their existence. And when, in time, it was learned that the northern part of the Asiatic continent was richer in game, they drifted toward it.

The animals moved north and east as the glacial ice retreated, and the people followed them in order to secure a steady supply of meat and furs. They followed them into Siberia, and then they went across into Alaska. Gradually they moved on southward.

Coon suggests that two main avenues of travel were open to them. One ran along the Pacific Coast; the other, along the eastern slope of the Rocky Mountains. Over these two great natural thoroughfares the people moved. Over them passed culture after culture. And each culture in turn distributed its own peculiar mores and systems of economics and industry and religious ritual.

There were no mass migrations over the Bering Strait land bridge. Being totally dependent on hunting and the gathering of wild vegetal foods for their existence, the immigrants were precluded from traveling together in large numbers for long

* *The Story of Man.*

distances. They moved in small bands, probably shifting no farther at one time than necessary to obtain needed sustenance. This does not mean, however, that constant shifting was always mandatory. Obviously, some wanderers were the nuclei of permanent populations in regions in which dependable and adequate quantities of food, fuel, and skins could be obtained.

The people who crossed from Siberia to the New World had no racial unity, for they had come from various parts of the Old World. Many of them carried blood strains and showed characteristics of Mediterranean, European, and African, as well as Asiatic, peoples. They spoke many tongues, displayed many cultural variations, and held many spiritual beliefs. All suffered the rigors and endured the exigencies of an extremely primitive life. However, those with a common bond, such as consanguinity, language, or other affinities, persisted in their efforts to remain united as much as possible. This is indicated by the existence of widely separated islands of people derived from one stock. Some Indians in the Southwest, for example, belong to stocks still inhabiting territories in Alaska and northern Canada.

The migrations from Siberia continued for an unknown number of millennia, probably a constant rivulet that may have diminished to a trickle at times but which never entirely stopped flowing. Meanwhile, as Charles Avery Amsden remarks,* lineal descendants of those who had already made the crossing

would be pushing along in their turn; not deliberately, not continually, but as the season favored and the lure of virgin territory

* *Prehistoric Southwesterners From Basketmaker to Pueblo.*

beckoned them on. Hunting folk drift easily, like the animals they hunt. So in the fullness of time all North America would get a sprinkling of human inhabitants . . . creeping as ink creeps through the blotter.

To which should be appended mention of some factors which acted as magnets, drawing them onward: the farther south they went the more temperate the climate became, the more hunting improved, the greater the profuseness and diversity of plants.

Probably most of the region now comprising the United States was nothing less than a hunter's paradise when the first Indians penetrated it. Scores of species of great Pleistocene animals ranged its luxuriant grasslands, its immense plains and mountains and forests. The people for thousands of years had no agriculture. They lived mainly by hunting, supplementing their meat diet with some wild vegetable foods. If it cannot be stated with certainty what plants the women gathered and prepared with their crude cooking methods, it can be asserted without question that the men were incredibly daring and competent killers of big game, such as mammoths and giant bison. Spear points found in the ancient bones of long extinct mammals tell the story.

Conjectures are not acceptable as evidence to scientists, yet they cannot refuse to consider them, for it often happens that imagination and theory open gates to the discovery of indisputable facts. The eminent Frank C. Hibben, who made numerous outstanding archeological discoveries, did not hesitate to write such imaginary scenes as the following: *

* *Was Ice Age Man a Game Hog?*

The elephant whirled and trumpeted shrilly as he sighted the men beyond the burning grass. One of the hunters fitted a long spear to his spear-thrower. Swinging his body into the cast, the man hurled the javelin. It struck high behind the mammoth's fore-leg. The flint point ripped through the inch-thick skin, shattering a rib, and bit deep into the lungs. A spout of blood blew out of the mammoth's trunk. The other men shouted, and rushed in for the kill.

The beast whirled to face them. His 10-foot-long tusks swept around. As a man closed to launch another spear, one tusk struck him on his side. In the same instant, the mammoth's trunk lashed at the man's head. His body broke like a shattered reed.

The animal thrust his tusks again and again into the shapeless mass that had been a human, but now other spears thudded into his chest. One flint point, striking low behind the foreleg, pierced the great heart. Blood pumped out of the gash. The mammoth swayed. He trumpeted once again, blowing a plume of blood above his back. Then, with a crash that shook the ground, the elephant fell on his side and died.

Now women who had been standing behind a line of bushes came forward. Some carried long flint knives. The men and the women together began to hack through the tough hide and butcher the carcass . . . they did not go near what was left of the hunter's body. . . . Death was a normal hazard of the hunt in America of 10,000 B.C.

The inchoate reasoning of primitive Indians assumed that a magic power was inherent in every living body and every object of nature, as well as in every attribute of these structures, that in any manner whatsoever affected the welfare of mankind. The Iroquois, for instance, called this fictive force *orenda,* and the Algonquian identified it as *manito,* two words by which it was known to early Europeans in the northeastern United States region. Later, white men would learn that the western Shoshoni spoke of it as *pokunt*, the Sioux as *mahopa*, and that there were names for it of corresponding significance in many other languages.

J. N. B. Hewitt wrote: *

this hypothetic principle was conceived to be immaterial, impersonal and mysterious in mode of action. It was limited in function and efficiency, not at all omnipotent, local and not omnipresent, and invariably embodied or immanent in some object. The conviction prevailed universally that it could be transferred, attracted, acquired, increased and suppressed by the *Orenda* of occult ritualistic formulas that were endowed with greater potency.

Speaking of the Five Nations of the northern Iroquois (Cayuga, Mohawk, Oneida, Onondaga, and Seneca), Hewitt stated: †

The religious activities of these tribes expressed themselves in the worship of all environing elements and bodies and many creatures of a teeming fancy, which, directly or remotely affecting their welfare, were regarded as man-beings or anthropic personages endowed with life, volition, and peculiar individual *orenda*, or magic power. In the practice of this religion, ethics or morals, as such, far from having a primary had only a secondary, if any, consideration. The status and personal relations of the persons of their pantheon were fixed and regulated by rules and customs similar to those in vogue in the social and political organization of the people, and there was, therefore, among at least the principal gods, a kinship system patterned on that of the people themselves.

* *Bulletin 30*, Bureau of American Ethnology.

† *Ibid.*

Through millennia, long before strangers from across the sea invaded their lands, American Indians believed all beings of their environment, and all the gods, major and minor, to be endowed with life, mind, and volition. They inferred, therefore, that the caprice of these beings and supernaturals could directly affect their relations with them. Thus, to obtain their needs they must gain the good will of hundreds of controlling mentalities by prayers, sacrifices, material offerings, and propitiatory acts.

The postulation of an imaginary dynamic force was necessary to the primitive Indian, for otherwise he could not have explained to himself the activities of life and nature.

It is improbable that a person of any race was more guided by spiritual beliefs than the primitive American Indian woman. Her beliefs influenced very nearly everything she did and everything she thought, day or night.

Speaking in general terms, her religion (indeed, the religion of all Indians) was reflective of a system of imitative and sympathetic magic aimed ritually at fulfillment of the requirements for life and living. It proffered no conception of a hereafter, such as the Heaven or Hell of the Christian doctrines. The abode of the dead, the final resting place of departed souls, was a blessed realm in which their spirits would forever dwell, but not without periodically returning, manifested in symbolism she understood, as bearers of beautiful thoughts and promising messages from the supernaturals who shaped the destinies of all living creatures. If there was grief, there was also inspiration in remembering.

The Indian woman saw herself as inextricably woven into the natural scheme of things. She was not simply bone and flesh, not simply the possessor of certain faculties. She was also of the sands, the winds, the stars, the plants, the thunder, lightning, rain, the sun and the moon and the seasons—everything that was born and lived and died in the indestructible, unvarying, and always balanced pattern of the universe.

A Potawatomi song, as recorded in translation by Alanson Skinner,* illustrates the universal belief in the unity of all things:

> *Now we all move, we're moving with this earth,*
> *The earth is moving along, the water is*
>   *moving along,*
> *The grass is moving, the trees are moving, the*
>   *whole earth is moving,*
> *So we all move along with the earth, keeping*
>   *time with the earth.*

In the Indian woman's theology, in addition to magic powers, gods possessed intelligence, emotions, and all other qualities and characteristics of humankind. Spirit beings, she believed, might, if they desired, intervene in every affair of her world, and they could be benevolent or malevolent as dictated by the whims or desires of the moment—the conception of a god that was all good was inconceivable to her—and she held determinedly to a conviction that all supernaturals would respond favorably to her prayers, her sacrifices, her appeals to their egos.

Her worship was not always expressed through a group ceremonial. She might have a totem sacred to her alone in her own thoughts, perhaps painted on a garment or represented on something she made with her hands, or even tattooed on her skin. She might seek to appease a deity by cleansing her body. And she might hope for a vision or reve-

---

* *Observations on the Ethnology of the Sauk Indians.*

lation from a spirit in answer to some desire—to cure an affliction, to give her courage and strength, to bring her success in some enterprise.

For her religion was not a thing apart from other aspects of life. It permeated every act—in planting seeds, in conceiving, in bearing children, in teaching and training her sons and daughters, in molding and decorating a simple pottery bowl, even in preparing for death.

2
Status

Pity the poor squaw,
Beast of burden, slave,
Chained under female law
From puberty to grave.

The anonymous author of these poetic lines was influenced by a misconception that from the earliest historical times to the present day has been harbored and disseminated by careless observers and uninformed persons.

Except among a few peoples whose social structures, religious dogma, and ceremonials were basically elemental and crude, the assertion that an Indian woman was an abject drudge of her tribe's men, both before and after marriage, is completely without foundation. An interesting correlative of this truth is the fact that most of the exceptions were peoples

27

who lived entirely by hunting and gathering wild plant foods, practicing no form of agriculture.

In tribes that were socially and politically advanced, whose ritual was highly developed, complicated, and unvarying in its formulae, women were not only highly regarded and protected but occupied positions of authority in both civil and ecclesiastical affairs. As previously stated, the spiritual hierarchies of many Indians included goddesses, but it should be noted also that on earthly ruling bodies were women who retained rights that had their fundamental source in the foundation of tribal society and government.

Invariably, when one seeks to determine the status of women in a particular aboriginal Indian tribe, one is confronted with irrefutable evidence that their rank was predicated upon certain premises: the conditions of the environment, the nature of the economy, the forms of social and political institutions, and the kind of domination exercised by the gods. None of these premises, however, may be construed as sufficient in itself, for each bears a relationship to the others; indeed, each was instrumental in creating the others.

Many of the largest and most important Indian peoples were matrilineal societies, that is, they traced descent through the female line. Among these were: in the East, the Iroquois, the Siouan tribes of the Piedmont and the Atlantic coastal plain, the Mohegan, the Delaware, various other tribes of southern New England, and the divisions of the Powhatan Confederacy in Virginia; in the South, the Creek, the Choctaw, the Chickasaw, the Seminole, and tribes of the Caddoan linguistic family; in the Great Plains, the Pawnee, the Hidatsa, the Mandan, the Oto, the Missouri, and the Crow and other Siouan tribes; in the Southwest, the Navajo, and the numerous so-called Pueblo tribes, including the well known Hopi, Laguna, Acoma, and Zuni.

Every member of these tribes belonged, either through birth or adoption, to a clan. In the clan lineal descent, inheritance of personal and common property and the hereditary right to public office and trust developed through the female line. Marriage between members of the same clan was prohibited.

In no case in the tribes maintaining the clan system were women without property rights, both the right of personal ownership and the right to dispose of personal belongings by giving or willing them to sons and daughters. Weapons and ceremonial paraphernalia belonged to men, but implements used for cultivating the soil, for preparing food, for dressing skins, for making garments and tipis, and other household articles belonged to women. In some tribes, raw materials, such as meat, corn, and skins, belonged to women. A woman could build and own a house, and among most people the lodge or tipi in which a family dwelt belonged to the mother. Only under the rarest of circumstances could the property of a woman be taken from her, and in most tribes she could under no condition be deprived of her possessions by her husband, even if their marriage was dissolved.

Outstanding examples denoting the high status of women come from the Pueblos of the Southwest, the Iroquois of the Northeast, and the Muskogean tribes (Creek, Choctaw, and Chickasaw) of the South.

Among most Pueblos, blood descent, and therefore membership in the clan and citizenship in the tribe, was traced through the mother. The home belonged to the mother, and her husband went to live in it; he did not take her to live in his home. Labor was equally apportioned between the sexes

insofar as possible. Gardens belonged to women and were inherited by their daughters. When a woman's daughters married, her sons-in-law came to reside with their wives in her
home. Pueblo men not only assisted their wives in domestic
duties, but made garments for them and wove blankets. The
Zuni woman occupied a particularly high status in the social
and political organizations of her tribe. A Zuni woman was a
member of The Rain Priesthood, which was composed of
nine persons and constituted one of the main religious
groups. Daughters, not sons, inherited the land owned by all
married Zuni men and women.

The clan systems of the Iroquoian and Muskogean tribes
were similar, if not identical, in many respects. Hewitt chose
a Mohawk term, *ohwachira*, as being best suited to describe
the primary unit of the clans of these two peoples. It signified "the family." *

The ohwachira was comprised of all the male and female
progeny of a woman, and of all her descendants in the female
line. The married women of child-bearing age of an ohwachira had the right to hold a council for the purpose of choosing candidates for chief and subchief of the clan of which the
ohwachira was a division. Usually the head of an ohwachira
was the eldest woman member. If a chief or a subchief were
to be deposed, the women's council of an ohwachira initiated
the action. All the land of an ohwachira was the exclusive
property of its women. The extreme power vested in an
ohwachira is illustrated by its authority to spare or take the
life of enemy prisoners captured in its behalf.

The early surveyor John Lawson † wrote that an Indian

* *Op. cit.*

† *History of North Carolina.*

man of North Carolina, presumably a Sioux, was considered most fortunate if he was

possessed of a great many beautiful Wives and Children, esteemed the greatest Blessings among these Savages, in which they have a true Notion.*

He also noted that when an Indian woman with children lost her husband in warfare or as a result of sickness, young men of her tribe or clan immediately came to her aid, cultivating and reaping crops for her, providing her with meat, fowls, and fish, repairing and refurbishing her dwelling when necessary, and doing heavy chores that she was incapable of performing.

An impressive number of the primary institutions of Indian peoples with social and political organizations that may be likened to those of the Iroquois—and there were many such tribes—were controlled by women. Hewitt provides the following list: †

Descent of blood or citizenship in the clan, and hence in the tribe, was traced through her. The titles, distinguished by unchanging specific names, of the various chieftainships of the tribe, belonged exclusively to her. The lodge and all its furnishings and equipment belonged to her. Her offspring, if she possessed any, belonged to her. The lands of the clan and so of the tribe, as the source of food, life and shelter, belonged to her. Burial grounds in which her sons and brothers were interred belonged to her. . . . As a consequence of the possession of these vested rights, the woman exercised the sovereign right to select from her sons the

* The subject of polygyny is treated in Chapter 7.

† *Op. cit.*

candidates for the chieftainships of her clan, and so of the tribe, and she likewise exercised the concurrent right to initiate the procedure for their deposition for sufficient cause. A mother possessed the important authority to forbid her sons going on the warpath, and frequently the chiefs took advantage of this power of the woman to avoid a rupture with another tribe.

The woman had the power of life or death over such alien prisoners as might become her share of the spoils of war to replace some of her kindred who may have been killed. She might demand from the clansmen of her husband or from those of her daughters a captive to replace a loss in her family.

There were chieftainesses who were the executive officers of the women they represented. These female chiefs provided by public levy or contributions the food required at festivals, ceremonials, and general assemblies, or for public charity.

It was also the duty of these women leaders to keep close watch on the course of affairs that affected the welfare of the tribe, to guard scrupulously the interests of the public treasury. They held the power to maintain the treasury's resources, which usually consisted of strings and belts of wampum, quill and feather work, furs, corn, meal, and other valuables that could be used to defray various public obligations, and they had a voice in disposing of the contents of the treasury.*

In reality there were neither bona fide kings nor queens among the Indians. A few chiefs may have held excessive powers, but the vast majority of tribes were almost pure democracies. White explorers, notably the English and Spanish, however, often mistakenly called influential Indian leaders "kings," and there are accounts of "queens" who al-

* The division of labor between men and women is discussed in Chapter 3.

legedly ruled their homelands. From the European point of view, at least, the application of the title "king" to a chieftain who was the head of a confederacy, or even of a powerful amalgamation of the branches of a single people, is understandable. The use of the title "queen" requires some explanation.

Every ohwachira had at least one of the politically influential women. Not infrequently a prominent woman who possessed extraordinary wisdom and leadership ability would be appointed regent in the event that an unexpected vacancy occurred in the office of a male chief who had gained his position through regular political channels. No cases are known in which a female regent became a permanent ruler of her people. Nevertheless, some early white chroniclers erroneously called these influential women "queens," and by the same mistake the title of "princess" frequently was bestowed on daughters of families ranking at the top of a tribal society.

Thus, in the narrative recounting Hernando de Soto's unrewarding search for gold, the chronicler, who called himself the Gentleman of Elvas,* writes of a "queen," or *cacica*, who governed an Indian "province," which undoubtedly was nothing more than a Creek settlement on the lower Savannah River in South Carolina. According to the account,

the *Cacica* came out of the town, seated in a chair, which some principal men having borne to the bank, she entered a canoe. Over the stern was spread an awning, and in the bottom lay extended a mat where were two cushions, one above the other, upon which she sate; and she was accompanied by her chief men, in other ca-

* He is believed to have been one Alvaro Fernandez of Elvas, Portugal.

33

noes, with Indians. She approached the spot where the Governor [De Soto] was, and, being arrived, thus addressed him:

"Excellent Lord: Be this coming to these shores most happy. My ability can in no way equal my wishes, nor my services become the merits of so a great a prince; nevertheless, good wishes are to be valued more than all the treasures of the Earth without them. With sincerest and purest good-will I tender you my person, my lands, my people, and make you these small gifts." *

The *Cacica* presented much clothing of the country, from the shawls and skins that came in the other boats; and drawing from over her head a large string of pearls, she threw them about De Soto's neck, exchanging with him many gracious words of friendship and courtesy.

Not far distant from the cacica's town were numerous large deserted villages, and De Soto was informed that two years earlier "there had been a pest in the land." This may have been the reason for the elevation of the cacica to political power. In any case, De Soto's men found some 350 pounds of pearls in the houses of the settlement, and he confiscated them. He further repaid her hospitality by permitting his men to "commit outrages" on the women, and by carrying her away

on foot with her female slaves. This brought us service in all the places that were passed, she ordering the Indians to come and take the loads from town to town.

After traveling with the expedition for several days, however, the cacica, using the excuse that she wished to go into a thicket to answer the call of nature, managed to slip away.

---

* The speeches which the Gentlemen of Elvas attributed to Indian leaders—and there were many of them—were the purest fiction, in each case manufactured for the occasion.

Some of her servants also escaped, and much to De Soto's irritation, they took with them a cane box "full of unbored pearls, of which those who had the most knowledge of their value said they were very precious."

Although royalty as it is construed in the worlds of other races was unknown among Indians, there were tribes in which social rank by classification existed. An incomparable example of Indian class distinction is that of the Natchesan people—the Natchez proper and two subdivisions, the Avoyel and the Taensa—who belonged to the great Muskogean linguistic family.

The three related groups dwelt in the lower Mississippi Valley and were descended from ancient people of the area, but they became notable in their own right. Probably about the beginning of the Christian Era they began to develop religious and social structures so different from those of surrounding tribes that their culture has been awarded an identity of its own, called Natchesan. Fortunately this culture reached its zenith shortly after the beginning of the historical period, and therefore the first explorers to enter the country of the Natchez people had an opportunity to write accounts of inestimable value to scholars.

The most significant characteristics of the Natchesan culture were an extreme form of sun worship, a highly complicated ritual, and the division of the society into suns, nobles, and commoners. There was also an additional group not even remotely consanguineous to any of the others—most probably composed of persons who had been captured in warfare or who had sought sanctuary among the Natchez—that was accorded no rank at all.

Omitting the unranked group, this was the Natchez social structure:

1—SUNS: children of sun mothers and stinkard (commoner) fathers.

2—NOBLES: children of noble mothers and stinkard fathers or of sun fathers and stinkard mothers.

3—HONORED PEOPLE: children of honored mothers and stinkard fathers or noble fathers and stinkard mothers.

4—STINKARDS: Children of stinkard mothers and honored fathers, or of stinkard fathers and stinkard mothers.

The Natchez were ruled by a male chief, regarded as a direct descendant of the sun, who enjoyed absolute power over the property and lives of his subjects. Obviously in such a social structure, women held no political powers, but there is no evidence to show that they were drudges or in any manner abused, and they could achieve high social rank. There was a certain disadvantage, however, in being a member of the large harem which the Sun Chief maintained. When he died his wives were put to death so that they might comfort him in the mysterious realm of the afterlife.

In the primitive philosophy of American Indians, deaths— especially those caused by accidents or otherwise untimely— as well as mysterious disappearances of tribal members were construed as the results of orenda,* or magic power exercised by some hostile agency. Except for a fortunate large increase in births, which they knew was unlikely, they saw adoption as the only effective means of countering this type of evil influence.

In both ancient and early historical times, therefore, adoption was an almost universal political and social institution. The fundamental purpose of the system was to offset human losses by restoring the dead and missing in the persons of

* See Chapter 1.

36

others, both male and female, who were either captured in warfare or acquired by merger.

Neither men, women, nor children who were officially adopted under prescribed ceremonials were relegated to lives of slavery. On the contrary, adopted persons became bona fide members of the family, clan, or gens adopting them, and thus, by this legal fiction, full-fledged citizens of the tribe to which these kinship groups belonged. Some Indians went so far as to believe—or at least to think it possible—that an adopted man or woman could embody the blood of the departed person he or she was chosen to personify among the living.

Except in a few regions, true slavery was not a common practice among Indians. Enemy prisoners were legitimate and valued spoils of war, and all tribes tried to obtain them, but only a few sought to hold them permanently and to benefit from their labors. Some peoples, notably several inhabiting the northeastern United States region, inflicted hideous tortures on a certain number of prisoners to glut savage passions, but by no means were all those taken so cruelly treated.

Women who fought in battle like warriors were slain without hesitation, but rarely, if at all, was the indiscriminate slaughter of women and children an objective of an attacking force. Normally, captured women and children were adopted by the victorious tribe. As most tribes practiced polygyny, women captives usually became wives of their male captors. It was possible for an adopted woman to be accorded great respect and to achieve high status. Illustrative of this possibility are historical events known to have occurred among the Navajo, a matrilineal tribe that at one time reputedly contained as many as sixty clans.

The Navajo took captive a great many women from Pueblo tribes, and a number of Navajo clans had their origin in a group of women from a single pueblo, or even from a single Pueblo woman. One Navajo clan is believed to have originated with a lone Spanish woman brought home by a Navajo raider.

The practical and materialistic Navajo, for whom banditry was a form of economy, saw only one way to develop for themselves the security and acquire the luxuries enjoyed by the Pueblos, whose culture was superior to and whose affluence greater than that of almost all Indian peoples living north of Mexico in the late prehistoric period. That way was to take from the Pueblos whatever they needed to augment their own fortunes, to raise their own standard of living, to improve their own welfare. While they stole from the Pueblos all manner of material things, they also took and retained male Pueblo craftsmen as teachers, and they made special efforts to capture young Pueblo women potters, weavers, and cultivators, not simply to serve them as workers but to bear children who could be taught the skills of their mothers.

Anthropologist Robert H. Lowie * wrote that among Indians of the Great Plains the

position of women was decidedly higher than is often assumed. An adulterous wife was liable to severe punishment and, as in all societies, instances of wanton abuse are on record, but these were definitely disapproved by public opinion. In cases of matrilocal residence the wife's relatives would protect her from arbitrary cruelty. A good woman enjoyed the esteem of her husband and of the community at large. . . . Institutional recognition of the wife's status is

* *Indians of the Plains.*

shown by the fact that among the Crow she took part jointly with her husband in sacred rituals.

To speak again of the Great Plains and prairie Sioux, while the Omaha, Ponca, Iowa, Kansa, and Osage are known to have had patrilineal clans, authorities are not agreed on the question with respect to the powerful Dakota and Assiniboin Sioux. The names of subdivisions that were known to early priests and voyagers, however, suggest that clans existed among the latter two tribes. Nevertheless, whether the Great Plains and prairie-woodland tribes were patrilineal or matrilineal, women's organizations or societies held important places in their social structures. There were women's auxiliaries of male military societies. There were societies for women of different ages, single women's societies, and widows' societies. There were guilds of women especially skillful in arts and crafts. There were women's societies that performed ceremonies designed to induce the gods to bless their people with good crops and good hunting.

The men of numerous Indian tribes believed that certain gods in the tribal religious hierarchy would give great attention to appeals from women. Therefore, a warrior intending to embark on a foray against an enemy might ask the members of some women's group to offer prayers for his success. If he returned victorious, he would customarily feast those who had "talked with the spirits" for him. Usually the requests of warriors under such circumstances were made to elderly women. In one case, at least, that of the Kiowa, an organization known as Forty Old Women was maintained for the purpose of interceding with various deities in behalf of men undertaking dangerous missions.

There were, of course, Indian tribes in which women held

few, if any, political or social rights, were forcefully subjected to excessive and exhausting labors, and were, in fact, relegated to the status of second-class citizens. For the most part, these were tribes whose cultures were basically simple and undeveloped in comparison with such highly complicated, progressive, and advanced civilizations as, for instance, those of the Hopewell people of the Midwest, the Anasazi and Hohokam peoples of the Southwest, and various ancient peoples of the South. It is interesting to note, moreover, that many of the tribes in which women were accorded only a low status, or none whatsoever, were nonsedentary, that few of them practiced any form of agriculture, and that almost all of them lived entirely on the bounties of nature, devoting themselves to an eternal hunt for sustenance in order to survive.

The Cree of the northern forests, the Shoshoni of the Rocky Mountains, and the Karankawa and Coahuiltecan of southeastern Texas might be cited as typical examples of tribes whose women were the slaves of men and who were accorded less consideration than chattels with some intrinsic value.

Lewis and Clark reported that a Shoshoni husband was the absolute proprietor of his wives and daughters, and might dispose of them by barter or in some other manner at his pleasure. Alvar Nunez Cabeza de Vaca, the first European to meet the Coahuiltecan and the Karankawa, wrote of them: *

Nothing is planted for support. . . . The men bear no burdens, nor carry anything of weight; such are borne by women and old men who are of the least esteem. . . . The women work very hard,

* *Relacion.*

40

and do a great deal; of the twenty-four hours they have only six of repose. . . .

Henry Rowe Schoolcraft, an ethnologist who spent half a lifetime among northern Indians, declared that Cree women were subjected to lives of

heavy and exacting toil . . . some mothers among them do not hesitate to kill their female infants to save them from the miseries which they themselves have suffered.*

In contrast to the dreadful comments, however, are many accounts by sixteenth- and seventeenth-century adventurers which mention the high degree of respect in which Indian women were held, remarking on their independence, relating how they were burdened with no more than a just share of responsibilities and obligations, and noting how they participated equally with their spouses in a harmonious community life.

A statement by William Bartram, who spent considerable time before the American Revolution among the southern tribes, typifies the more pleasant reports regarding the status of Indian women. Praising the high character and agreeable disposition of the Muskogean people, he said: †

I have been weeks and months amongst them, and in their towns, and never observed the least sign of contention or wrangling; never saw an instance of an Indian beating his wife, or even reproving her in anger. . . .

* *Personal Memoirs.*

† *Observations.*

And he added:

indeed their wives merit their esteem and the most gentle treatment, the women being industrious, frugal, careful, loving and af-
fectionate.

White settlers in early colonial times saw that invariably an
Indian man preceded his squaw when walking along a road,
a trail, or in a village, and so the legend was born that the
squaw was inferior in social status to the man, her lord and
master, and therefore was required to show her respect by
keeping behind him. In reality, the custom had nothing
whatsoever to do with ethics, protocol, or rank. When walking or entering a community or a lodge, an Indian man went
ahead of his squaw expressly for the purpose of protecting
her from unexpected danger—in Indian idiom, "to make the
way safe for her."

A justifiable conclusion seems to be that in the vast majority of the hundreds of prehistoric American Indian tribes,
whether their social structure was patrilineal, matrilineal, or
bilateral, women not only enjoyed well-defined prerogatives,
but among a very large number wielded considerable social,
religious, and political powers.

3
Duty

They all work together to build the villages, the women being engaged in making the mixture and the walls, while the men bring the wood and put it in place. . . . The men spin and weave. The women bring up the children and prepare the food.

—Pedro de Castaneda, describing the Pueblos, 1540

The division of labor and responsibilities between men and women cannot be conclusively set forth in a way that would be applicable to all primitive Indian peoples.

In general, upon men rested the duties of protecting wives, children, other relatives, and material possessions, of repelling raiders, and of guarding tribal lands and hunting grounds against intruders. As all Indians lived in almost constant danger of attack, the men, whether at home in a temporary camp or on the march, were required to be prepared night and day for defensive combat. Conversely, men went away to war, for glory and plunder, or to gain revenge for a harmful incursion by an enemy. Although men did most of the hunting, they were by no means the sole providers of sustenance for their families.

In general, upon women rested the duties of the household, of caring for the children, of preparing and cooking food, of dressing skins, sewing, ministering to the ill and aiding the crippled and wounded, making clothes and mats and sleeping robes, packing for travel or to accompany the men on a hunt, butchering, weaving cloth and baskets, making pottery—a countless number of obligations.

However, the duties of women were not all of the domestic kind. Women were required to cultivate, and in desert regions to irrigate, to gather nuts and berries, seeds and grasses, and roots and other edible wild plant foods as well as useful fibers, to fish, and even to snare small animals and birds. The spring planting in a garden or a field was done exclusively by women, for it was believed that inasmuch as they possessed and controlled the faculty of reproduction, seeds sown by them would be more fertile and would produce better and larger crops than seeds planted by men.

Beyond, and in many respects within, these general categories, the sexual division of labor and responsibilities varied greatly among tribes. If universally the norm was basically the same, it was as universally affected and changed by local conditions, by needs peculiar to a people or an environment. There could be no inflexible patterns, no hard and fast lines of demarcation. Exigencies, traditions, customs, religious beliefs, even climate were sources of innumerable deviations.

The ethnologist Frederick W. Hodge thought "the division of labor was not so unequal as it might seem to the casual observer."

He found it "difficult to understand how the line could have been more fairly drawn in a state of society where the military spirit was so dominant." *

It is the view of the anthropologist Harold E. Driver that the

classic picture of the lazy Indian brave and the industrious squaw applies only to certain cultural areas, and even there demands considerable qualification. In regions where hunting and warfare loomed large, as on the Plains, the Prairies, and in the East, a man performed his most strenuous duties away from home.

The violent nature of these activities, which usually were accompanied by religious fasting, exhausted the men engaging in them, and it was necessary to spend some time resting and recuperating from their ordeals.

Wrote Driver:

Most of the early historical observers in those areas saw only village life, where the women actually were doing most of the work. The result was a distorted picture.†

In all tribes women were assisted in their work, both in the home and in the field, by young people, by men unable to hunt or engage in warfare because of injury or advanced age, and in some cases by slave-servants. The large number

* *Bulletin 30*, Bureau of American Ethnology.

† *Indians of North America.*

of women's games and sports and societies enumerated in scientific studies makes it clear that most Indian women enjoyed not a little relief from arduous and routine duties. They attended what might be termed sewing bees, vied in quilling and weaving contests, and took part in numerous ceremonials and social functions from which men were excluded. A game of shinny in which a hair ball covered with buckskin and a curved stick were used was widely played by women. In another common women's game, a ball was thrown with a long rod on whose end was a skin loop. In this contest a player was not permitted to touch the ball with the hands. It may be safely assumed that women also found time to engage in the popular pastime of gossip.

In the region that now embraces California, Oregon, and Washington, in the southern and eastern woodlands, in a relatively small part of the Southwest, and in the lower Missouri Valley area, the work of building habitations was performed largely, and in some sections entirely, by men. Among many prairie peoples of the Midwest, and notably among the buffalo-hunting tribes of the Great Plains, making tipis and constructing dwellings of earth, poles, and thatch was an obligation of women. In the high arid country, inhabited by the Pueblos, Navajo, and some other tribes, the work of house-building was about equally divided between the sexes.

Women were both the architects and the builders of earth lodges, grass houses, and tipis, three types of habitations used by many primitive peoples in the central prairies and Great Plains regions. Their skill in constructing these functional dwellings, which were so well adapted to the respective areas in which they prevailed, was nothing less than remarkable. Two eminent ethnologists, Alice C. Fletcher and

James Mooney, who made exhaustive studies of early Indian habitations, provide authoritative information regarding the materials and the methods of construction employed by the ingenious women builders.*

The earth lodge, according to Fletcher,

was a dwelling partly underground, circular in form, from 30 to 60 feet in diameter, with walls about six feet high, on which rested a dome-shaped roof with an opening in the center to afford light within and to permit the egress of smoke. The entrance was a projecting passageway from 6 to 14 feet long.

The method of construction was first to draw a circle on the ground and excavate the earth within it from 2 to 4 feet deep. About one and a half feet within the circle were set crotched posts some 8 or 10 feet apart, on which were laid beams.† Outside these posts were set others, one end of them braced against the bottom of the bank of earth at the periphery of the circle, and the other end leaning against the beams, forming a close stockade, an opening being left at the east side for the entrance.

Midway between the center of the excavation and the stockade were planted 4, 6 or 8 tall crotched posts, forming an inner circle. In the crotches were laid heavy beams to support the roof. The bark was stripped from all the posts and beams.

The roof was formed of long, slender, tapering tree trunks, stripped of bark. The large ends were tied with strings of the inner bark of the elm to the beams at the top of the stockade, and the middle to those resting in the crotches of the inner circle of posts. The slender ends were cut so as to form the circular opening in the center of the roof, 2 or 3 feet in diameter. Outside this framework

* *Bulletin 30*, Bureau of American Ethnology.

† Even in areas in which women were chiefly or entirely responsible for constructing dwellings, men helped in raising heavy beams and posts and in other work requiring great strength.

branches of willows were placed close together across the posts of the wall and the beams of the roof, and bound tightly to each pole, beginning at the ground and continuing upward to the central opening.

Over the thatch was placed a thick coating of sods, cut so that they could be lapped, and laid like shingles. The wall and roof were afterward carefully tamped with earth and made impervious to rain. The long entranceway was built in the same manner as the lodge, and thatched and sodded at the same time.

The grass of the sod continued to grow, and wild flowers brightened the walls and roof of the dwelling. The blackened circle around the central opening in the roof, produced by the heat and smoke, was the only suggestion that the verdant mound was a human abode.

Within, the floor was made hard by a series of tampings, in which both water and fire were used. The fireplace was circular in shape and slightly excavated. A curtain of skin hung at the opening from the passageway into the lodge. The outer door was covered with a skin that was stiffened by sticks at the top and bottom, which was turned to one side to give entrance to the passageway.

The couches of the occupants were placed around the wall, and frequently were enclosed by reed mats which could be raised or lowered.* More than one family sometimes occupied a lodge, and in such case the families took different sides. The back part, opposite the entrance, was reserved for the keeping of sacred objects and the reception of guests.

In the winter curtains of skin were hung from the beams of the inner circle of posts, making a smaller room about the fireplace. The shields and weapons of the men were suspended from these inner posts, giving color to the interior of the dwelling, which was always picturesque, whether seen at night, when the fire leaped up and glinted on the polished blackened roof and when at times the

* Most furnishings also were made by women.

48

lodge was filled with men and women in their gala dress at some social meeting or religious ceremony, or during the day when the shaft of sunlight fell through the central opening over the fireplace, bringing into relief some bit of aboriginal life and leaving the rest of the lodge in deep shadow.*

Ceremonies attended the erection of an earth lodge, from the marking of the circle to the putting on of the sods. Both men and women took part in these rites. This type of dwelling was used by the Pawnee, Arikara, Omaha, Ponca, Osage, and other tribes.

Fletcher, an expert on Pawnee culture, described the special significance of the earth lodge to this people: †

Among the Pawnee are preserved the most elaborate ceremonies and traditions pertaining to the earth lodge. These tribes are said to have abandoned the grass house of their kindred at some distant period and, under the teaching of aquatic animals, to have learned to construct the earth lodge. According to their ceremonies and legends, not only the animals were concerned with its construction—the badger digging the holes, the beaver sawing the logs, the bears carrying them, and all obeying the directions of the whale—but the stars also exercised authority.

The earlier star cult of the people is recognized in the significance attached to the four central posts. Each stood for a star—the Morning and Evening stars, symbols of the male and female cosmic forces, and the North and South stars, the direction of chiefs and the abode of perpetual life. The posts were painted in the symbolic colors of these stars—red, white, black, yellow. During certain ceremonies corn of one of these colors was offered at the foot of the post of that color. In the rituals of the Pawnee the earth lodge is

* Even with care and regular repairs an earth lodge rarely could be made to last for more than two generations.

† *Ibid.*

made typical of man's abode on the earth; the floor is the plain, the wall the distant horizon, the dome the arching sky, the central opening the zenith, dwelling place of Tirawa, the invisible power which gives life to all created beings.

Tipi is a Siouan word, deriving from the root *ti,* meaning "to dwell," and *pi,* meaning "used for." Men may have cut the poles and shaped the wooden pegs for it, but women constructed it; moreover, they usually took it down, packed it on a travois pulled by dogs, and reerected it when traveling.

Mooney states that

the typical tipi of the Great Plains people, when first seen by white men, consisted of a circular framework of poles brought together near the top and covered with dressed buffalo skins sewn to form a single piece, which was kept in place by means of wooden pins and ground pegs.

It commonly had about 20 poles, averaging 25 feet in length, each pole being hewn from a stout sapling, usually cedar, trimmed down to the heart wood. The poles were set firmly in the ground so as to make a circle of about 15 feet in diameter, and were held together above by means of a hide rope wound around the whole bunch about 4 feet from the upper ends, leaving these ends projecting above the tipi covering. There were 3 main poles, or with some tribes 4, upon which the weight of the others rested.

The cover of the tipi consisted of from 15 to 18 buffalo skins dressed, cut and fitted by women in such a way that, when sewn together with sinew thread, they formed a single large sheet of nearly semi-circular shape. This was lifted into place against the framework by means of a special pole at the back of the structure, after which the two ends were brought around to the front and there fastened by means of 8 or 10 small wooden pins running upward from the doorway nearly to the crossing of the poles. The lower border was kept in place by means of pegs driven into the ground at a distance of about 2 feet apart around the circle.

The tipi doorway faced the east, the usual door being a piece of dressed skin stretched over a rectangular or elliptical frame, frequently decorated with porcupine quills or other ornaments. The dressed skin of a panther, coyote or buffalo calf, with the hairy side outward, was sometimes used.

The fire pit was directly in the center, and the smoke escaped through the opening in the top, at the crossing of the poles. By means of movable skin flaps on each side of the smoke hole, the course of the smoke could be regulated as the wind shifted.

There were commonly 3 beds or seats, one at each side and one at the back of the tipi, each consisting of a long platform covered with a sort of mat of light willow rods, over which were thrown buffalo robes or blankets. The head end of the mat usually hung from a tripod in hammock fashion. Decorated curtains above the beds kept off the drops of water which came through the smoke hole in rainy weather. The ground was the floor.

In warm weather the lower part of the tipi cover was raised to allow the breeze to pass through. In cold weather the open space around the bottom was chinked with grass.

The tipi was renewed every one or two years, its completion being the occasion of a dedicatory ceremony, and those of prominent families decorated with heraldic paintings and other ornaments.

The grass house was used largely in the southern Great Plains by the Caddoan tribes (except the Pawnee). It resembled an immense beehive. Fletcher called it

a comely structure. Skill is required to build it, and it has an attractive appearance both without and within. It adapted to a warm climate only.

In describing the materials used and the methods of construction employed by the women builders, Fletcher wrote:

Its construction was begun by drawing a circle on the ground, and on the outline setting a number of crotched posts, in which beams were laid. Against these, poles were set very closely in a row so as to lean inward; these in turn were laced with willow rods and their tops brought together and securely fastened so as to form a peak.

Over this frame a heavy thatch of grass was laid and bound down by slender rods, and at each point where the rods joined an ornamental tuft of grass was tied. Two poles, laid at right angles, jutting out in four projecting points, were fastened to the apex of the roof, and over the center, where they crossed, rose a spire, 2 feet high or more, made of bunches of grass.

Four doors, opening to each point of the compass, were formerly made, but now, except when the house is to be used for ceremonial purposes, only two are provided, one on the east to serve for the morning, and one on the west to go in and out of when the sun is in that quarter. The fireplace was a circular excavation in the center of the floor, and the smoke found egress through a hole left high up in the roof toward the east.

The four projecting beams at the peak pointed toward and were symbolic of the four points of the compass, which were the paths down which the powers descend to help man. The spire typified the abode in the zenith of the mysterious permeating force that animates all nature. The fireplace was accounted sacred; it was never treated lightly even in the daily life of the family.

With few exceptions, among tribes that depended in large part on horticulture for their subsistence, the division of labor was grossly inequitable, with women performing most of the work of sowing, cultivating, harvesting, and storing. This was especially true in the East, the South, the Midwest, the eastern half of the Great Plains, and the southeastern part of the Southwest. In some sections of the Southwest, however, men were the chief farmers. Once again the Pueblo tribes were an exception, agricultural labors being about equally divided between men and women. Horticulture was not practised on the Pacific slope before the arrival of the white man; the Indians of that region subsisted entirely on game, fish, shellfish, and wild plant foods. Nor did the buffalo-hunting peoples of the high Great Plains engage in farming, but they made annual journeys to barter wth sedentary tribes of the Missouri Valley for maize.

The implements with which Indian women worked in the fields were extremely crude, but obviously the desired results were obtained by using them. Accounts of explorers, traders, and missionaries are rife with reports of flourishing fields of maize, beans, squash, and other products. Hoes, choppers, and digging tools were made of wood, flint, tortoise shells, and the shoulder blades of large animals. Seeds were dropped into holes made in the ground with pointed sticks or planted in small, handmade mounds.

It should be noted that even in localities in which the field work was done principally by women, they were not burdened with all tasks related to horticulture. Customarily men performed the heaviest labor, such as ground breaking, clearing thick underbrush and logs from plots to be cultivated, and transporting products to rock-lined cellars and other types of storehouses. On the midwestern prairies, in the East, and in the South, even though open meadows abounded in these regions, much, if not most, of the farming was undertaken in woodlands, for it was in them that the softest grounds were to be found. The prairies of Iowa, Illinois, Indiana, and adjacent sectors, which are the best lands for corn today, could not have been worked with the crude Indian tools. Without plows and draft animals the tough sod could not have been broken and turned. Driver describes the preparation of the woodland farms:

Large trees were not felled but were simply girdled by pounding with a stone axe. This treatment was sufficient to kill the tree and permit the sun to shine through its bare branches. Another way was to pile brush around the trunk and set it on fire.*

All work connected in any way with subsistence, whether done by men, by women, or by both together, was either preceded or followed by some type of religious observance. In almost every region there were planting rites, wild-food-gathering rites, and harvest rites. Frequently throughout the growing season appeals were made to the gods who controlled the elements for rain and favorable weather. Even the clearing of ground was accompanied by a ceremony designed as an apology to the spirits of plants that were killed. For example, a Mississippi Valley Indian quoted by William Jones explained: †

We do not like to harm the trees. Whenever we can, we always made an offering of tobacco to the trees before we cut them down. If we did not think of their feelings, and did not offer them tobacco before cutting them down, all the other trees in the forest would weep, and that would make our hearts sad, too.

Although hunting of large animals was done by men, women played important roles in hunting ritual. Not a few of the ancient ceremonials have survived to this day, even in

* *Op. cit.*

† *Ethnography of the Fox Indians.*

areas in which the killing of game is rigidly controlled by state and federal laws. Underhill recounts how, only a few years ago, she stood in the plaza of a pueblo on a dark January morning

to watch the Mother of Game bring in the deer. It was almost dawn when we heard the hunter's call from the hillside. Then shadowy forms came bounding down through the pinon trees. At first we could barely see the shaking horns and dappled hides. Then the sun's rays picked out men on all fours, with deerskins over their backs and painted staves in their hands to simulate forelegs. They leaped and gamboled before the people while around them pranced little boys who seemed actually to have the spirit of fawns.

In their midst was a beautiful Pueblo woman with long black hair, in all the regalia of white boots and embroidered *manta*. She was their owner, the Mother of Game. But she was also Earth Mother, the source of all live things including men. She led the animals where they would be good targets for the hunters, and, one by one, they were symbolically killed.*

Lowie writes of very old traditional ceremonials with similar significance that were held by two women's organizations of Upper Missouri River tribes, the Goose Society and the White Buffalo Cow Society: †

The Goose women performed ceremonies in order to make the corn crop prosper and to attract buffalo herds. The White Buffalo Cow women were also called upon to lure buffalo. They wore a feathered headdress of albino buffalo skin in hussar fashion and

* *Red Man's Religion.*

† *Indians of the Plains.*

danced in position, raising each foot alternately higher than the other and waddling from side to side.

The journal of William Clark of the Lewis and Clark expedition contains a vivid description of a Mandan ceremonial in which young hunters invoked the mysterious powers believed to be possessed by fertile women and old men in an appeal to end adverse hunting conditions:

When buffalo becomes scarce they send a man to harangue the village, declaring that the game is far off and that a feast is necessary to bring it back, and if the village be disposed a day and place is named. . . . At the appointed hour the old men arrive, and seat themselves crosslegged on skins round a fire in the middle of the lodge with a sort of doll or small image, dressed like a female, placed before them. The young men bring with them a platter of provisions, a pipe of tobacco, and their wives, whose dress on the occasion is only a robe or mantle loosely thrown round the body. On their arrival each youth selects the old man whom he means to distinguish by his favour, and spreads before him the provisions, after which he presents the pipe and smokes with him.

The young men, who have their wives back of the circle, go each to one of the old men with a whining tone and request the old man to take his wife, who presents herself naked except for a robe, and have sexual intercourse with her. The girl then takes the old man, who very often can scarcely walk, and leads him to a convenient place for the business, after which they return to the lodge. If the old man returns without gratifying the man and his wife, he offers her again and again. . . . All this is to cause the buffalo to come near so that they may kill them.

Under normal circumstances in the East, the South, the middle prairies, and the Southwest, where crops were grown and stored and numerous types of edible plants and fruits were seasonally available, obtaining her share of her family's sustenance could hardly be termed difficult for an Indian woman. People dwelling on or adjacent to the seacoasts could obtain various kinds of sea foods throughout the year. The Pacific coastal region, with a mild climate, normally provided bounteous supplies of vegetal foods, fruits, and nuts. True, tedious labor was often required, and all of these regions at times suffered from shortages caused by such adversities as drought, pestilence, excessive rains, and unusually heavy snows. And in the northern country eastward from the Rocky Mountains to the upper Great Lakes, in which winters were invariably long and severe, the early spring was very often a period of great hardship and want. Women made a practice of putting aside hides with some meat left on them. When bellies were empty and the children began to cry because they were receiving insufficient nourishment, these hides could be scraped and the frozen bits of meat boiled. In times of dire need, the hides themselves could be cut up, cooked, and eaten.

Woman's day began with the dawn, and if all of her duties were not burdensome, she seldom knew moments when some work was not awaiting her. If there was no cooking to be done, or plants to be gathered and berries and nuts to be harvested, there was a basket or a pottery utensil to be finished, moccasins and clothing to be made, hides to be tanned, and skins to be decorated with quills and feathers and painted designs, and there were children to be trained, and dances and ceremonials in which she was required to participate.

In many tribes dancing took up a considerable part of a woman's time, and it was seldom done simply for pleasure.

The dances were fraught with symbolism and mystic meaning, and it was incumbent upon a woman to perform them not only competently but with strict compliance to rules that had come down through generations. A mother was responsible for teaching her daughters the steps peculiar to every dance, the correct attitudes to display, and the significance of each rite in which women took part.

Grinding, grinding, grinding—a ceaseless task of women in all regions. Archeologists have found manos, or grinding stones, among the artifacts of some of the oldest Indian cultures. Before maize reached tribes north of Mexico, some seven thousand years ago, women ground seeds and nuts and various dried plants. It is probable that since that ancient age through historical times Indian women spent more hours in grinding wild and cultivated foods than in any other work.

The smaller grinding stones were held in the hand, and were usually unshaped fragments of stone. The larger ones were slabs, boulders, or fragments which rested on the ground or were held in the lap while in use. In many localities exposed surfaces of rock were utilized. Except for the smallest and lightest types, grinding stones could not be transported from place to place; therefore, tribes who traveled on hunts, perhaps for weeks or even months, kept grinding stones at various locations along the routes of their wanderings.

As Casteneda demonstrated, the practice of piping soothing music into factories is by no means an invention of modern-age psychologists. Writing of the Pueblos, he depicted this domestic scene of 1540:

They keep the separate houses where they prepare the food for eating and where they grind the meal, very clean. This is a separate room or closet, where they have a trough with three stones fixed in stiff clay. Three women go in here, each one having a stone, with which one of them breaks the corn, the next grinds it, and the third grinds it again. They take off their shoes, do up their hair, shake their clothes, and cover their heads before they enter the door. A man sits at the door playing on a fife while they grind, moving the stones to the music and singing together.*

* See Winship.

4
Food

*Their food is generally boiled maize, mixed with kidney beans.
. . . Also, they frequently boil in this pottage, fish of all sorts,
either taken new or dried, as shad, eels, alewives or a kind of
herring, cut in pieces bones and all. I have wondered many times
that they were not in danger of being choked with fish bones; but
they are so dexterous in separating the bones from the fish in their
eating thereof that they are in no hazard. Also, they boil in this
frumenty all sorts of flesh, as venison, beaver, bear's flesh, moose,
otters, raccoons, etc. . . . . Also they mix with the said pottage
several sorts of roots. . . .*

*—Daniel Gookin, describing Indians
in Massachusetts, 1674*

No diet of today anywhere in the world is more nutritious
than was that of primitive Indians under normal circum-

stances. Meats, vegetables, fruits, nuts, and fish were consumed in well-balanced proportions in most parts of the United States region.

The greatest difficulties regarding food supplies with which Indians had to contend were created by the vagaries of nature. Customary and beneficial subsistence patterns frequently were disrupted by unfavorable weather, by drought or abnormal precipitation, or by excessive heat or prolonged cold. These meteorological phenomena caused game shortages and prevented wild plants from maturing.

Yet, Indians were not ignorant of ways to preserve many types of food—quite to the contrary. Agricultural tribes built cribs, bins, silos, and earth cellars, and used natural rock caves in which maize, nuts, dried squash and pumpkins, beans, and roots or tubers could be safely stored in winter. Meat of big game, such as buffalo, elk, and deer, was thinly sliced and dried on racks, an entrée to which white plainsmen would give the name jerky. Indian pemmican, a combination of dehydrated meat and animal fat, was, in Tom McHugh's opinion,* "the products of one of the most effective methods of food processing ever devised."

One of the earliest accounts of Indians' preparation of jerky and pemmican was that of Castaneda,† who was among the Plains Apache of eastern New Mexico and northern Texas in 1540:

These people dry the flesh of the cows [bison] in the sun, cutting it thin like a leaf, and when dry they grind it like meal to keep it and make a sort of sea soup of it to eat. A handful thrown into a

* *The Time of the Buffalo.*

† See Winship.

pot swells up so as to increase very much. They season it with fat, which they always try to secure when they kill a cow.*

If to the taste of the Spaniards with Coronado pemmican was a bit unsavory, they were thankful that it could be obtained, for when it was flavored with wild cherries or some other seasoning, even plain salt, it relieved to some extent the monotony of their fare. However, they could not bring themselves to partake of two other dishes which the Apache appeared to relish. Castaneda writes of them:

The Indians empty a large gut and fill it with blood, and carry this around the neck to drink when they are thirsty. When they open the belly of a cow, they squeeze out the chewed grass and drink the juice that remains behind, because they say that this contains the essence of the stomach.

The advantages of pemmican over jerky are expertly explained by McHugh: †

Although it [jerky] weighed only about one sixth as much as fresh meat, it was bulky—rather like a bundle of tree bark. In rain or damp air, it absorbed moisture readily, gaining weight as well as molding or decaying, often both. And if completely dry, it was hard to eat, calling for strong teeth and endless munching.

These drawbacks were eliminated by pemmican. McHugh states:

* Castaneda was not among these people long enough to understand that the fat made it possible for them to preserve meat for an indefinite period, for years, if necessary.

† *Op. cit.*

After pulverizing jerky, the Indians packed it into bags sewed from buffalo rawhide, each one about the size of a pillow case. Into these sacks they poured hot liquid marrow fat, which seeped through the contents to form a film around each crumb of meat. The bags were stitched up at the mouth and sealed with tallow along the seams. Before the contents had time to harden, each bag was tramped or pressed into a flat shape about six or seven inches thick. A single sack, weighing about ninety pounds, was known as a "piece" of pemmican, and made a convenient parcel for back-packing or portaging. It was also easy to store; placing a row of pieces on rocks or small logs to keep them off the ground, the Indians piled up the remaining sacks like cordwood. . . . Plain pemmican, if properly made with only dried lean meat and rendered fat, lasted almost indefinitely.

Several thousand years before the advent of the Christian Era, Indian women were serving corn (maize) to their families and guests in a great variety of dishes. No other plant indigenous to the New World was more nutritious, could be prepared in a larger number of ways, or could be palatably combined with as many different types of foods. It could be boiled, toasted, baked, fried, and roasted in the ear; mixed with meats, fish, other cultivated vegetables, and countless species of wild plants, fruits, and nuts; ground into flour for breads and cakes; added to thicken soups; and used as a main ingredient of almost any kind of stew. Samp, a maize porridge, hominy, succotash, and pone were Indian inventions.

Oddly enough, maize was not a native of the United States region. It was ingeniously domesticated in southern Mexico and Central America from wild relatives. How long it took primitive botanists to complete the difficult process, of course, can never be determined. Domesticated maize approximately seven thousand years old has been found in southern Puebla, Mexico.

64

While it is apparent that maize was brought north from Mexico, undoubtedly over ancient Indian trade trails, any estimate of the time of its arrival in the United States region would be pure conjecture. However, some light was thrown on the mystery by an archeological discovery made in 1948. In that year, two distinguished botanists, Paul S. Mangelsdorf and C. Earle Smith, Jr.,* were excavating in Bat Cave, New Mexico. On a low level of the rock shelter they came upon ears of maize. That in itself might not have been considered an unexpected finding, but laboratory analysis disclosed that the Bat Cave maize was more than five thousand years old. It was both a pop corn and a pod corn. The ears were not enclosed in husks.

After the initial discovery, a much newer type of maize was found in Bat Cave. The cobs and kernels were larger, and it had a husk similar to modern corn. It was given a date about A.D. 1. Here was evidence of long cross-breeding to improve yield. Indian folklore, if not scientific discoveries, give support to the conclusion that several millennia before the discovery of the New World maize had become a main Indian staple in the Southwest, the Southeast, the Midwest, the East, and some relatively small areas of the middle and southern Great Plains.

RECIPE

How one kind of Indian cornbread, sometimes called corn cakes, was made by prehistoric women:

The corn was picked in the milky stage, shucked, and the kernels scraped from the cob. The kernels were ground on a stone metate until they were a creamy mush. Salt was added.

---

* See bibliography.

The mush was formed with the hands into cakes several inches in length, two or three inches wide, and about an inch in thickness. They were then wrapped in corn shucks that had been made soft and pliable by steeping in hot water.

A pit nine inches to a foot deep was dug in the ground, and a fire was built in it. When the walls and floor of the pit were thoroughly heated, the fire was raked out. The wrapped corn cakes were placed in layers in the pit, and covered with wet corn husks. They were then covered with a mixture of hot ashes and earth, and a small fire was built over the pit. The corn cakes were ready to eat after several hours of slow baking in this earth oven.*

Beans were second in importance to maize among plants cultivated by primitive Indians of this country, and squash ranked third. Several varieties of each were grown. Like maize, both beans and squash were first domesticated in southern Mexico or Central America, whence they were brought to the American Southwest, and perhaps from the West Indies to the Southeast, by migrating Indians or trading groups. Domesticated beans estimated to be six thousand years old and remains of domesticated squash dated at least a thousand years older by the radio carbon method were found in the Ocampo Caves of Tamaulipas, Mexico. Evidence that provides a reliable timetable for the northern diffusion of either beans or squash has not been discovered, but it is believed that beans reached the Southwest as early as

---

* Navajo women called these cakes "kneel down bread," because they carefully folded the shucks over the dough with the narrow ends tucked under, which suggested to them a person kneeling. The recipe was followed by women of many other tribes, and the cakes were called by numerous names, none that we know of, however, so imaginative as this.

five thousand years ago. Sunflowers were domesticated by Indians north of Mexico, but they were comparatively unimportant as a food source, the seeds being used almost entirely as a flavoring.

An account of all the wild plants gathered for food by prehistoric Indian women would be too long for inclusion in this volume. Donald R. Kirk lists more than three hundred edible plants for the western United States, and there were undoubtedly as many, if not more, in the Midwest, South, and East.*

Maize, beans, and squash were not cultivated by Indians of the Pacific Coast, and the people of this region depended to a large extent on wild plants, roots, berries, and nuts, especially acorns, to supplement a diet consisting essentially of fish, shellfish, oysters, and small game. Seafood was also an important food on the Gulf of Mexico and the Atlantic Coast. However, in only two or three small areas did wild plants equal game as a source of food.

Indian women were well informed as to the comparative values of foods; they knew the nutritional benefits to be derived from certain plants and the dangers inherent in unbalanced diets. They knew that the finest food of all was meat, but that meat alone did not answer all the demands of the body. Whatever they may have called protein, if indeed they defined it at all, they knew that its greatest source was meat. Thus, few meals were prepared without meat in some form, and among agricultural tribes, meats were usually served with maize or beans, secondary sources of protein. They understood as well, however, that other elements were needed to sustain good health, such things as starches,

* See bibliography.

sugars, and fats. Many plants, both wild and domesticated, contained these substances. As Driver notes,* "the sugars and starches of wild plants were indispensable in areas where game was scarce and farming absent or little developed. . . ."

But it might be added that wild plants provided valuable food elements in all areas, especially nuts, berries, and roots.

Among tribes of the Northwest Coast, salmon was the pièce de résistance, although they consumed many other kinds of fish. Salmon was filleted, dried, and stored in great quantities. Agriculture was not practiced, and wild vegetable foods were comparatively unimportant in the native diet of the peoples living immediately on the coast or on the lower reaches of rivers. However, throughout the entire Northwest, the camas, a plant botanically related to the hyacinth with a highly nutritive, edible bulb, was a staple. Women dug out the roots in open prairies, where the camas grew in great profusion. Various kinds of berries were fairly abundant and were harvested in season. For storing in the Northwest, states Philip Drucker: †

berries were cooked to a pulpy mass, poured into rectangular wooden frames lined with skunk-cabbage leaves, and dried into cakes. Another storing technique was to stir them into a mixture of year-old olachen [candlefish], grease and cold water. . . . In addition to being boiled in watertight baskets or boxes, food was steam-cooked in large shallow pits filled with hot stones by placing it on the stones and covering the whole affair with leaves or mats, then pouring water through to the stones.

* *Indians of North America.*

† *Indians of the Northwest Coast.*

Acorns were one of the chief foods of perhaps 75 per cent of the primitive tribes of California. Women gathered them in baskets. They could be dried and stored for long periods. For consumption they were cracked, pulverized, sifted, leeched, and boiled with hot stones in a tightly woven utensil. The resulting gruel, according to A. L. Kroeber,

was about as tasteless as wheat flour cooked in water would be, nearly as nourishing, but richer in starch, and when prepared from certain species, perceptibly oily.

The commonest method of leeching acorns of their tannin, he states,

was to pour hot water over the meal as it lay spread out in a basin of clean sand. Cold water also apparently removes the bitterness if given time enough. Thus, acorns buried for a year in swampy mud come out purplish and are ready to be roasted on coals.*

The most valuable of all wild animals was the shaggy beast commonly called buffalo. It ranged chiefly from the Rocky to the Allegheny Mountains, from Canada to Mexico. As is said of the domesticated hog, virtually every part of the buffalo—more properly called the bison—was used by Indians except the snort, and even that sound was imitated in hunting ceremonials. Mention has been made of pemmican, but buffalo meat was also baked, boiled, and roasted. Tongues, eyes, brains, tripe, hearts, and other internal organs were eaten. Blood and fat went into puddings, stews, soups, and other dishes. Fetal calves, when very small, were considered a

* *Indians of California.*

great delicacy. Bone marrow, extracted by cracking large, roasted bones, was savored by all Indians. Some relished lungs boiled with corn. Others were especially fond of grilled udder, with or without the milk in it.

The first white man to write of *Bison americanus* was Nunez Cabeza de Vaca. In his invaluable *Relacion*, printed in Spain in 1542, he said:

Cattle come as far as here [Texas]. Three times I have seen them and have eaten of their meat. I think they are about the size of those in Spain. They have small horns like the cows of Morocco; the hair is very long and flocky like the merino's. Some are tawney, others black. To my judgment the flesh is finer and fatter than that of this country [Spain].

RECIPE

Many years ago, according to McHugh, an extremely elderly Hidatsa woman told an anthropologist how to make Buffalo Blood Broth: *

"To obtain a base, she tapped blood from a pool that settled between the lungs and diaphragm of a slain bull (throwing away the clotted blood, which was difficult to cook and likely to spoil the broth). Pour one and a half to two gallons of blood into a large kettle. Add one cup water, one piece of buffalo marrow-fat twice the size of an egg, and two handfuls of dried cooked squash. Bring to a boil. Prepare a stirring paddle from a two-foot length of chokecherry sapling, fringing the bark at one end to render a cherry flavor. Prepare another stick by stripping the bark from a small twig. Dip this into broth and remove. If red blood clings, continue boiling. Broth is ready to serve when stick emerges clean and white."

* *Op. cit.*

Throughout the Prairies of the Midwest and the Great Plains, innumerable varieties of seasonal wild plant foods were available. Two of the most popular were onions and turnips, for besides being savory, they could be mixed with other foods and they could be dried and stored. Strawberries, Juneberries, gooseberries, artichokes, buffalo berries, cherries, plums, roseberries, and other types ripened in turn.

Royal B. Hassrick writes: *

Berry-picking was a family affair, generally the job of young unmarried girls and old women. Picking aprons were worn by some, while others picked into their upheld skirts. For fruit like buffalo berries, cherries, or gooseberries, which grew on bushes, the picker placed a small hide beneath the bush and dropped the harvest onto it. The supply could then be transferred to skin bags. The women usually brought a dog and travois to transport the harvest. . . . Men were not exempt from gathering vegetables. When an abundance was discovered, a husband and wife might pick together so that the greatest possible amount could be preserved before spoilage occurred. . . . The Sioux women so thoroughly surveyed the potentials of native plant life that literally no source of food was overlooked. Indeed, it was a common practice for the old women to probe new campsites in search of a mouse's cache of dried beans.

Indians in almost every part of this country could obtain fowl in great quantities at some time of the year. Three or four main flyways crossed the United States region from north to south, and in the spring and fall immense flocks of ducks and geese migrated over them. Passenger pigeons darkened the skies of the prairie lands. The Pueblos main-

* *The Sioux.*

tained large flocks of domesticated turkeys, and wild turkeys in great numbers were native to the South and Southeast.

The tribes of the East enjoyed a varied menu of fish, game, maize, and many types of wild fruits, berries, and plants. They used tuckahoe and other fungi for food, and tuckahoe bread was commonly consumed from Massachusetts to Georgia, as well as in other sections of the South. Throughout New England sugar and syrup were obtained by evaporating maple sap.

Many Indian women mixed certain clays with foods that were excessively bitter or contained acid to make them edible. For example, Alfred F. Whiting * cites the Hopi, who

eat a salty clay with the wild potato and the berries of *Lycium*. This particular clay has the property of counteracting the acid which would otherwise make the foods inedible.

Natural supplies of sugar were scarce, and sometimes almost nonexistent, in arid areas. It was obtained in numerous ways. The Hopi method was probably similar to customs of many tribes facing the problem. Whiting notes that among the Hopi

wild grasses were allowed to sprout and were then ground. The resulting meal was chewed by the women who spit it out in a bowl. This mixture of starch and saliva produced a satisfying if not over sanitary supply of sugar. Cactus fruits, and dried squash are also said to have been prized as sweet flavorings.

The Sioux are commonly thought of, and usually portrayed, as great warriors of the northern Great Plains, but

* *Ethnobotany of the Hopi.*

for an unknown number of millennia they were people of the midwestern woodlands and prairies. Their first identifiable homeland was composed of parts of Ohio, Kentucky, Indiana, Illinois, and Tennessee. They dwelt in this region in the stage which archeologists call Archaic, and which began about ten thousand years ago. It was a time when animals of the Pleistocene, such as mammoth, sloth, giant bison, and other Ice Age species, were still hunted, although their numbers were rapidly diminishing and they would soon become extinct.

It was an incredibly bountiful land after the Pleistocene mammals had vanished from it, indeed, an Indian paradise. Wildfowls inhabited its marshes in countless millions. In the woodlands and prairie meadows lived an endless variety of game. A network of rivers, large and small, contained mussels in incredible quantity, and it is these bivalve mollusks that are of particular interest in this narrative.

The culture of the Archaic Period Siouans is called Indian Knoll. The name was selected with good reason. The knolls were not natural elevations. They were created by the discarded shells of mussels which the Indians had consumed.

These shell mounds were located along the river shoals, where mussels were most abundant. The villages of the people stood on them. The shells as well as the bones of animals and birds were thrown about the campsites and cooking fires. Apparently, as the refuse mounted about them, the Indians moved their fragile dwellings a few feet or a few yards to prevent their view of the surrounding areas from being obscured. This is indicated by the size of the shell mounds. Some of those discovered were spread over from three to seventeen acres and ranged in height from four to twelve feet. Obviously there is no way of determining how many years or how many shells were required to create mounds of such great dimensions. It can be said, however, that these ancient Siouans were very fond of mussels.

RECIPE

How to make sofki, *a thin, sour gruel prepared by Creek and other southern Indian women from corn, water and lye:*
Pound the corn into a coarse meal. Fan it with feathers to remove broken grains and husks. Put two quarts of the meal into a gallon pot of hot water. Place it over a fire and allow to boil. Fill a perforated vessel with clean wood ashes. Pour water on the ashes to form a lye. Allow the lye to percolate through the ashes into the meal and water, which will gradually turn yellow. Keep water on the mixture for several hours. When the mixture has become very thick, remove from fire and allow to cool. Add pounded hickory nuts and marrow. This improves the flavor. Serve sofki in mugs, with a plate of blue dumplings, a very palatable cornmeal preparation.

The region of the United States was, for the most part, a land of plenty. There were two areas, however, in which hunger was a way of life. One was the Great Basin, which embraced much of Utah, all of Nevada, and parts of Oregon and California. The other included the barren, arid reaches of south Texas, inland some distance from the Gulf of Mexico coast. In these desolate sectors, men, women, and children spent virtually every hour of the day in a desperate struggle to obtain enough seeds and roots, rodents, rabbits, mice, snakes, and insects to keep themselves alive. They were the Western Shoshoni of northwestern Utah and central and northeastern Nevada, the most unproductive parts of the Great Basin, and the Coahuiltecan of South Texas and northern Mexico. Understandably, in these wretched domains the women had little time to participate in ceremonials of any kind, and any rituals that were performed were no more than pitiful pleas to the gods for food.

Early French fur hunters called the Gosiute and other bands of western Shoshoni *les dignes de pitié,* or "those who deserve to be pitied." The celebrated explorer and religious, de Smet, wrote of them: *

There is not, very likely, in all the universe a more miserable, more degraded and poorer people. The land they inhabit is a veritable waste. They lodge in crevices of the rocks, or in holes dug in the earth; they have no clothing . . . they range the barren plains in search of ants and grasshoppers, on which they feed, and they think it a feast when they come upon a few tasteless roots or nauseous grains. . . . They eat the corpses of their kindred, and sometimes even their own children.

The historian Hubert Howe Bancroft pictured them in these words: †

Lying in a state of semi-torpor in holes in the ground during the winter, and in spring, crawling forth and eating grass on their hands and knees, until able to regain their feet; having no clothes, scarcely any cooked food, in many instances no weapons, with merely a few vague imaginings for religion, living in the utmost squalor and filth, putting no bridle on their passions, there is surely room for no missing link between them and the brutes.

* See Chittenden.

† *Native Races.*

The Coahuiltecan lived in a forbidding land of great dry reaches, immense sweeps of stunted growth and thorny shrubs. Large game animals were extremely scarce on the arid plains of south Texas, and even small animals were not plentiful. There were some deer, antelope, and javelina, and there were rabbits, reptiles, birds, and various insects, but there were not enough of any species of animal to provide them with adequate and assured supplies of meat. They lived largely on wild plant foods, and they were no less than ingenious in making good use of cacti, mesquite, beans, nuts, sotol, agave, and other vegetable growths. Nunez Cabeza de Vaca, the first European to write from personal experience about the south Texas Indians, said of them:

Occasionally they kill deer, and at times take fish; but the quantity is so small and the famine so great, that they eat spiders and the eggs of ants, worms, lizards, salamanders, snakes, and vipers that kill whom they strike; and they eat earth and wood, and all that there is, the dung of deer, and other things that I omit to mention. . . . They save the bones of the fishes they consume, of snakes and other animals, that they may afterwards beat them together and eat the powder. . . . To them the happiest part of the year is the season of eating prickly pears; they have hunger then no longer, pass all the time in dancing, and eat day and night. While these last, they squeeze out the juice, and open and set them to dry, and when dry they are put in hampers like figs. . . . The peel is beaten to powder.

So far as is known, all Indians preferred cooked food. Wild plant foods, of course, required cooking to make them digestible. But among a great many people freshness was not a rigid requirement. In fact, both meats and vegetal foods were permitted to advance toward putrefaction before being consumed, some tribes possessing a distinct preference for them in this condition. The accounts of explorers, traders, and missionaries tell of seeing Indians, both men and women, butchering a carcass they had come upon, roasting or boiling the rotting meat, and eating it with relish. There are numerous stories relating how hunters pulled drowned animals that were bloated and partially disintegrated from rivers, butchered them, and carried the putrid flesh to their camp, even though there was no shortage of live game in the country about them.

Father de Smet, the first religious to reach many parts of the American West, described how some Assiniboin women prepared a feast at which he was a guest:

If a bit of dried meat or any other provision is in need of being cleansed, the dainty cook fills her mouth with water and spurts it upon the object.

A certain dish is prepared in a most singular manner, and they are entitled to a patent for the happy faculty of invention. The women commence by rubbing their hands with grease, and collecting in them the blood of the animal, which they boil with water. Finally they fill the kettle with fat and hashed meat. But—hashed with the teeth! Often half a dozen old women are occupied in this mincing operation for hours; mouthful after mouthful is masticated, and thus passes from the mouth into the cauldron, to compose the choice ragout of the Rocky Mountains.

Add to this, by way of an exquisite dessert, pulverized ants, grasshoppers and locusts that have been dried in the sun. . . .

Apache women, even though their people occupied a country in which precipitation was moderate at best, provided a remarkably varied diet. Except in the worst desert areas, big game was fairly abundant throughout Apacheria.

The Apache hunted only to fill needs, never killing animals for sport. Although they were available, fish, bear, and beaver were not consumed, a custom the genesis of which is not known but which was undoubtedly due to cosmogonic and religious views that had long been forgotten before the arrival of the Spanish. While deer, antelope, elk, and bison were preferred to other game, cougar, rats, hares, wolves, coyotes, squirrels, lizards, and snakes were eaten. Caterpillars were an ingredient of one type of gruel, and dishes containing blood and bone marrow were common. Certain parts of the viscera of large animals were considered tidbits. Wild fowl were not a staple, but were used on occasions of dire need, such as those which might be caused by reverses in warfare or unsuccessful raids. The Apache obtained a number of nourishing foods from wild plants. Among these were several species of cactus fruit, pinon nuts, bulbs and roots of many kinds, mesquite beans, mushrooms, greens, berries, acorns, and seeds.

It was customary in many tribes to eat only two meals a day, but all efficient Indian women with social responsibilities were prepared to serve visitors at any time—unless warfare or some other emergency disrupted affairs—with tasty hors d'oeuvres, such as salmon eggs and other species of roe, thin slices of raw buffalo liver, wild bird eggs, small pieces of raw fish garnished with onions, sunflower seeds, cracked hickory and other nuts, crumbs of dried deer heart or beaver tail, and perhaps a stimulating cup of fermented cactus juice.

5
Crafts

These [blankets] are like shawles, some of them made from the inner bark of trees, and others of a grass resembling nettle, which, by treading out, becomes like flax. The women use them for covering, wearing one about the body from the waist downward, and another over the shoulder, with the right arm left free.

—Description of Creek women, De Soto expedition, 1540

In the two villages . . . there was some very beautiful glazed earthenware with many figures and different shapes. Here they also found many bowls full of a carefully selected shining metal with which they glazed the earthenware. . . . In all these provinces they have earthenware glazed with antimony and jars of extraordinary labor and workmanship, which were worth seeing.

—Description of Pueblo pottery, Coronado expedition, 1540

The women of the Southwest, notably those of sedentary tribes, were the most expert and artistic prehistoric potters north of central Mexico.* They made ceramic vessels in practically every form known to primitive peoples, ranging from large cooking and storage pots to delicately molded and beautifully painted and decorated jars, bowls, platters, bottles, ladles, and box-shaped utensils.

The question arises: When and from whom did they acquire this craft in which they became so highly skilled?

People to whom archeologists have given the name Basket Makers, and who were immediate predecessors of the pueblo builders, dwelt at the beginning of the Christian Era—and probably several centuries earlier—in the Four Corners region, which is comprised of parts of the present states of Colorado, Utah, New Mexico, and Arizona. They did not have true pottery, and most archeologists believe that the whole concept of clay containers came to them from other people. Perhaps, but other theories are worthy of brief consideration. H. M. Wormington and Arminta Neal state that the Basket Makers †

did have some sun-dried clay dishes. These usually contained a vegetable temper or binding material, such as cedar bark, to prevent cracking, and were molded in baskets. It is not known whether the idea of pottery, but not the technique for producing it through firing, had reached the Basketmakers from some other people, or if the idea of making the sun-dried dishes was one which they developed themselves. . . . it is not impossible that the idea developed from the practice of putting clay in baskets while con-

* Indeed, the Pueblo women of today still retain this commanding position.

† *The Story of Pueblo Pottery.*

structing cists. If clay were left for some time in a basket it would naturally harden and, if the center portion had been scooped out, the hardened residue in the basket would produce a vessel of sorts.

C. A. Amsden * believes:

Something like this probably did happen, many times over. . . . We do know that fragments of thick mud dishes, molded in baskets, have been found in Basketmaker caves in which not a single scrap of true fired pottery came to light. They were not residual coatings of clay, but fashioned vessels, deliberately made. Their insides were smoothed, their outsides plainly stamped with the imprint of the basket which shaped their form.

Many burned ruins of Basket Maker dwellings have been found, and in them were crude mud dishes that had been turned to true pottery by the destructive flames. This suggests the possibility that Basket Makers may have discovered by accident that firing clay vessels turned them into semistone and made them more durable. The idea must remain in the realm of pure speculation. Moreover, there is considerable evidence to indicate that knowledge of pottery manufacturing in all regions north of Mexico was acquired through cultural diffusion.

Long before the Basket Maker period, pottery-making was a highly developed art in South America and Mexico. That trade trails existed between South and Central America and the United States region many centuries before the beginning of the Christian Era is unquestionable. Knowledge and ideas came north over them as well as products. People in northern Mexico and southern Arizona possessed pottery

* *Op. cit.*

probably as early as 1000 B.C. But other people living some two thousand miles to the east of them possessed it much earlier.

The first drastic cultural transition that archeologists have been able to record in the area of the southeastern coasts began about 2700 B.C. Then, and within the span of a few years thereafter, pottery appeared at various places. Of the greatest significance is the fact that it was also the first pottery known to have reached the area of the United States.

It was given the name Stallings Island ware, after the Georgia site where the oldest examples were found. For years the origin and development of the type puzzled scientists, but at last some of them came to believe that the mystery had been solved. Stallings Island pottery undoubtedly came from South America. The conclusion makes mandatory the consideration of what anthropologist Carleton S. Coon appropriately termed "the trans-Pacific problem."

For, in the opinion of James A. Ford and other archeologists, Stallings Island ware is similar in some traits to ancient Japanese pottery. And this particular type of ceramic—called Valdivia—apparently was first introduced on the coast of Ecuador some five thousands years ago.

The possibility that voyagers from Japan reached South America as early as 3000 B.C. seems remote, but it cannot be ignored. The prevailing winds sweep in a great arc eastward across the northern Pacific. The voyage westward would have been easier. In a daring adventure, Thor Heyerdahl proved that men sailing on a raft of the type used by Peruvian Indians could reach the Polynesian Islands. Moreover, he found ancient Peruvian pottery on Easter Island, where it was pre-Polynesian.

Prehistoric South American and Caribbean Indians made

long voyages on trading missions to Cuba, Haiti, Jamaica, and many other islands, and along the coasts of Colombia, Panama, Guatemala, and Mexico. They could easily have reached the mainland of the southern United States from many of these places. Evidently their pottery did reach it, if not on direct voyages then by transfer from people to people along the way.

Two types of decorated pottery soon emerged in Florida from the first undecorated Stallings Island ware. Called Tick Island and orange incised, they have traits indicating their derivation from pottery found in northern South America, which in turn has traits found in Ecuador's Valdivia pottery. Thus, an unbroken chain of diffusion seems to have been established, indeed a very old and very long chain running from Japan, across the Pacific to Ecuador, and by land and up the coasts by water to the southernmost areas of the United States. There is good reason to believe, as well, that Indian emigrants from Asia brought pottery to North America over the Bering Strait to Alaska, from where it was transported southward over various routes.

Pottery making was a craft which permitted the primitive Indian woman any number of opportunities to express individual artistry. She might use the basic manufacturing technique commonly employed by potters of her tribe—either coiling, modeling or molding—but no method demanded conformity in any respect. She was free to give an odd shape to a pot or bowl; nothing precluded her from being inventive; and she enjoyed the prerogative of choosing whatever decorative patterns or colors most pleased her at any given time.

The coiling method was the most widely used. After the base of a vessel was shaped with the hands, the walls were built by coiling on sausagelike pieces of clay and fused with either the fingers or a paddle. The sides were prevented from caving by some form of anvil held inside the pot. If the modeling method was used, the sides of the pot were formed with slabs of clay attached to the base and fused by pinching with the fingers. In the molding method, clay was shaped around some type of mold, perhaps a stone, a piece of wood, or a smaller piece of fired pottery especially made for the purpose.

Pottery, almost entirely the work of women, provides for archeologists the most useful cultural record of any left by aboriginal peoples. As Martin, Quinby, and Collier point out: *

Pottery vessels may break into hundreds of pieces, but each fragment retains its identity . . . pottery vessels and shreds are not subject to the destruction of erosional and chemical forces within the ground. They long outlast such perishable objects as those made of wood, bark, fiber, and animal skin.

Material and chemical analysis make it possible to identify a piece of pottery, even a fragment, as belonging to a certain tribe, or at least as having come from a specific area of the country. As in every other product of primitive Indians, religious symbolism was present in the designs which women painted on pottery.

Thousands of years before Indian women of the United States region knew anything about making pottery, they were weaving baskets. The materials used, exclusively vegetable fibers, were perishable, but in extremely dry sites in the deserts of the American Southwest, fairly well preserved

* *Indians Before Columbus.*

basket fragments have been found that laboratory tests indicate were in use in 7000 B.C., and possibly two millennia earlier.

The first explorers of every region found basketry a highly developed craft. There is no data even hinting that weaving baskets originated in a certain geographical area or was an invention of the women of one tribe. Techniques and designs undoubtedly were diffused through cultural exchanges, but scientists almost invariably can determine by the type of weaving and the materials used in a basket the locale in which it was manufactured.

Primitive women employed three major weaves in making baskets, bags, and mats. These were coiling, twining, and plaiting. Plaiting was the method most commonly used in the East, South, and the larger part of the Midwest. Both twining and coiling were used in the Southwest, some parts of the Great Plains, the Rocky Mountain region, and the southern half of California. Along the northwest Pacific Coast the twining method was predominant.

No matter what method a woman used, however, a finished basket was reflective of individual creativity and artistry, as were mats, bags, boxes, and other articles woven of fibers. Designs were not taught, nor were specifications or patterns decreed by tradition; they were, as Clark Field states,* "created by the individual weaver."

He adds that the weaver

Must first develop a manner of weaving that will form a shape adequate for the basket's final use. She must then find suitable materials in her area for this weaving project. This step completed, she

* See bibliography.

mentally creates a decorative design and invents a method of weaving it into the basket.

Women of numerous tribes wove baskets with such fineness and tightness that they would hold water and could be used in cooking by dropping hot stones into them. Baskets with fitted lids, standing three or four feet in height, and with diameters of two or three feet, were made for storing maize, nuts, and other dried foods. Baskets of every conceivable size and shape were made for utilitarian uses, such as trays, serving dishes, and receptacles in which personal belongings, jewelry, ornaments, and small tools and utensils were kept. There were large and small baskets used only in religious ceremonies, and there were trays on which gambling games were played.

Otis T. Mason states: *

Basketry, including wattling, matting and bagging, may be defined as the primitive textile art. Its materials include nearly the whole series of North American textile plants, and the Indian women explored the tribal habitat for the best. They knew the time and seasons for gathering, how to harvest, dry, preserve, and prepare the tough and pliable parts for use and to reject the brittle, and in what way to combine different plants with a view to the union of beauty and strength in their product.

The basket maker's tools were her highly skillful fingers, fingernails for gauge, teeth for a third hand or for nippers, a stone knife, a bone awl, and polishers of shell or gritty stone. The inner bark of cedar, elm, birch, pine, and other trees was widely used in weaving. It was torn into strips, shred-

---

* *Bulletin 30*, Bureau of American Ethnology.

ded, twisted, and spun. From it were made twine, yarn, rope, mats, baskets, dishes, buckets, and bags. In the Southeast, baskets were made of cane and hickory splints, and the art was highly developed. Reeds and tules of many species were used from ocean to ocean for mats and baskets. In the Northwest, Indian women used cedar bark, spruce roots, and a variety of tough grasses.

Although the women of many tribes were competent and artistic basket makers, most archeologists consider the basketry of the California Pomo to be the finest and most beautiful made by any primitive people in the world. The Pomo women employed both the coiling and twining methods, working with willow, pine root, sedge root, and redbud. They obviously did not think of basket making as a utilitarian routine, but as an art with unlimited possibilities.

Kroeber * described some of the finest Pomo baskets as

splendidly showy. Black, wavy quail plumes may be scattered over the surface . . . or fine bits of scarlet from the woodpecker's scalp worked into a soft brilliant down over the whole receptacle. . . . The height of display is reached in the basket whose entire exterior is a mass of feathers, perhaps with patterns in two or three lustrous colors.

Some of the most beautiful baskets had edges of beads and fringe of evenly cut haliotis shells. For the Pomo these served as gifts and treasures. No higher use could be made of these magnificent works of art than to destroy them in honor of a loved one or a distinguished person who had passed away.

The true loom was not known to primitive Indian women

* *Indians of California.*

weavers, but had the discovery of America been delayed perhaps less than a century, its development might well have occurred. In the majority of tribes weaving was done by hand, without the aid of apparatus. However, in at least three widely separated regions, parts of the Atlantic coastal plain, the Aleutian Islands, and some sections of the Southwest, the warp was suspended from tree limbs or some other type of support. Here was the first step toward creation of a loom. But it is believed that Europeans, notably the Spanish, taught Indians to use the handloom, and development of the fixed upright and horizontal looms followed in due course. Driver * notes that the

earliest descriptions of looms among Indians of the Southeast appeared more than a century after the beginning of white settlement, and, therefore, derivation of the loom in that region from other American areas or from Europe should not be ruled out. On the other hand, the inner-bark mantles observed by the De Soto expedition were woven so finely that they were sometimes mistaken for cotton. Work of such high quality suggests the true loom.

Spinning was known to all tribes. One ancient method widely used was to roll fibers between the palm and thigh. But many primitive weavers employed some form of spindle whorl.

The Pueblos of the Southwest, among the finest Indian weavers, had three types of looms, and one or more of them may have existed in a crude stage of development before historical times. However, it is definitely known that after the advent of Spanish colonization the Pueblos were using waist

* *Op. cit.*

looms and vertical and horizontal looms. The Hopi produced fine woven blankets and garments, but in contrast to other southwestern tribes, the men did most of the weaving. Navajo myths relate that they learned to weave from the greatest weaver of all, Spider Woman. But, of course, they learned the art from the Pueblos, who for many centuries before the arrival of the first Spaniards had been superb weavers of native cotton. Navajo women, who were skilled basket makers, became the great weavers of their people, developing an industry that not only supplied the needs of the tribe but produced blankets and other woven articles for trade that were widely distributed at a good profit as far east as the Great Plains.

The feather coats of Carolina Indians, said Lawson,*

are very pretty, especially some of them, which are made extraordinary charming, containing several pretty figures wrought in feathers, making them seem like a fine flower silk-shag . . . others are made of the green part of the skin of a mallard's head, which they sew perfectly well together, their thread being either the sinews of a deer divided very small, or silk grass.

Mason † states that

at the time of the discovery . . . the Indians were found weaving into blankets feathers and down of birds as well as rabbit skins cut into narrow strips. The strips of skin were twisted into rolls as thick as a finger, and the shafts of feathers were caught between the

* *Op. cit.*

† *Op. cit.*

strands of twine in twisting. These fluffy rolls constituted a kind of warp, held in place by rows of twined weaving of stout cord. . . .

Not only the soft skins of small animals and feathers were used in blankets and other articles. Until white settlement destroyed the buffalo in the East, Indian women made good use of buffalo hair, and for two centuries afterward it was skillfully utilized by weavers of the Great Plains tribes. McHugh states: *

Some artisans spun the [buffalo] wool into strands for weaving blankets, scarves, bags, wallets, and—in combination with porcupine quill stiffeners—women's girdles. Strands were twisted or braided into ropes, which served as halters, lariats, belts, and cords. A Shoshoni halter examined by Meriwether Lewis contained six or seven strands woven into a cord "about the size of a man's finger and remarkably strong."

Skin dressing by Indian women achieved a level of excellence comparable to that of any primitive people of the world. The list of articles manufactured from animal skins is extremely long, but mention may be made of some of the most important products: shirts, coats, pants, skirts, dresses, bags, trunks, robes, bedding, cases, baskets, moccasins, medicine pouches, boxes, blankets, headbands, girdles, wallets, dog saddles, straps, shields, quivers, parfleches, and tipis.

Many garments worn by aboriginal Indians would be greatly envied by modern-day women, for they were made of such valuable and beautiful skins as beaver, otter, badger, mink, ermine, and marten. The most useful and the most

* *Op. cit.*

widely used hides were those of the buffalo, the deer, the elk, and the antelope. More durable products could be made from the hides of these four animals than from any others; for warmth such skins as wolf, coyote, and bear served as well; and the easily workable skins of such small animals as foxes, rabbits, squirrels, gophers, muskrats, prairie dogs, and the fine furs mentioned above, among others, were most useful for ornamentation and decorative purposes, although Indians inhabiting areas in which big game was scarce made entire garments of small skins.

The methods employed for dressing skins were similar throughout the region of the United States, the main difference being in the chemicals used. Primitive Indians did not use tannic acid, insofar as is known, even though many tribes ate acorns, an important source of this agent. In the tanning process, use was made of a cooked mixture of brains and liver, grease of various types, pounded soapy roots, decoctions of bark, solutions of mixed corn and eggs, corn pulp, animal broth, urine, and both warm and cold water.

Because the Indian women of Great Plains tribes continued to use their traditional method of tanning long after contact with whites, valuable details of the process have been recorded by careful observers. The noted ethnologist James Mooney states that this process consisted of six principal stages: fleshing, scraping, braining, stripping, graining, and working. A different tool was required in each stage. A number of hides were usually dressed at the same time, and the women worked together out of doors.*

According to Mooney, the fleshing process was begun as soon as possible after the hide was stripped from the carcass.

* *Bulletin 30*, Bureau of American Ethnology.

The hide was staked out on the ground, fleshy side up, and usually two women scraped off the flesh and fat by using a gouge with a serrated edge made from the leg bone of a large animal. The next stage, scraping, involved a very laborious process. Several women worked together, each using a short adz made of wood or elk horn and having a stone blade set at right angle to the handle. The hide was staked out with the hair side up. An old dressed skin was placed beneath it to break blows and to keep the dressed surface clean. Each side was dressed in turn.

In the braining process, which followed next, the skin was thoroughly anointed with one or more of the mixtures listed above. Some women added a little salt at this point. After the braining was completed, a bundle of dried grass was placed in the center of the hide and saturated with hot water, and the corners were then brought together over it in bag fashion. The skin was tightly twisted into a solid ball, and hung up to soak overnight.

In the stripping stage the dampened hide was opened out and then twisted into a rope in order to expel moisture. The hide was then stretched in a frame made of a crosspiece and two stout forked poles. The lower end was staked to the ground. The hide thus stretched stood at an angle of forty-five degrees. Now two women did the stripping, using a tool with a stone blade which resembled a small hoe. As this instrument was drawn from top to bottom it caused water to ooze out. When one woman neared the bottom her partner followed the same track before moisture could work back into the skin.

After the stripping of the entire hide was completed in this manner, it was left on the frame to dry and bleach. Graining came next. This was done with a globular piece of bone cut from the spongy portion of the humerus of a large animal. With this tool the hide was rubbed as with sandpaper, which reduced it to uniform thickness and smoothness and removed any hanging fibers. If breaks or holes had appeared, they were repaired with an awl and sinew thread.

The final stage, called working, was performed to make the skin soft and pliable. This was accomplished by drawing it for some time in seesaw fashion across a rope of twisted sinew stretched between two trees. Some Indians worked the skin by drawing it over the top of a thick post smoothed for this purpose, or around a tree trunk. Two women always worked together, one at each end of the skin. When the desired pliability and softness had been attained, the skin was cleansed with a wash of white chalk clay in water, applied with a brush made of root fibers or grass. When the chalk solution had dried to a powder, it was brushed off.

As previously noted, Indian women made the tipis. The remarkably high quality of the skins used in them is attested to by a passage in the account of an expedition commanded by Vincente de Zaldivar among Apaches of the southern Great Plains in 1598. Zaldivar and his Spanish soldiers

came upon a rancheria [settlement] of fifty tents made of tanned skins which were very bright red and white in color. They were round like pavilions, with flaps and openings, and made as neatly as those from Italy. They are so large that in the most common ones there is ample room for four individual mattresses and beds. The tanning is so good that even the heaviest rain will not go through the skin, nor does it become hard. On the contrary, when it dries it becomes as soft and pliable as before.

Zaldivar bartered for one of these amazing tipis and took it with him, and even though it was so large, as has been stated, it did not weigh more than fifty pounds.

Zaldivar's chronicler continues:

To carry these tents, the poles with which they set them up, and a bag of meat and their pinole, or maize, the Indians use medium sized, shaggy dogs, which they harness like mules. They have large droves of them, each girt around the breast and haunches, carrying a load of at least one hundred pounds. . . . It is both interesting and amusing to see them traveling along, one after the other, dragging the ends of their poles, almost all of them with sores under the harness. When the Indian women load these dogs they hold the heads between their legs. . . . they travel at a pace as if they had been trained with fetters.

Although it would be demonstrated early in historical times that the soil and climate of the South were favorable for growing cotton, it was not cultivated by the aboriginal inhabitants of that region. It seems obvious that if some wild variety of this plant had grown there, the highly intelligent Indians, such as the Creeks, Chickasaw, Choctaw, Sioux, and other tribes, would have found a means of utilizing it. The earliest observers, however, say nothing of native cotton. Archeologists believe that the cotton blankets seen by members of the De Soto expedition among Indians on the lower Mississippi River reached there through trade channels from the Southwest.

It is known that in the arid region that now comprises Arizona and New Mexico, cotton has been cultivated and woven into cloth for a great many years, perhaps for several millennia. Like maize and other crops, it was grown with flood irrigation or by hand watering. Cloth, cord, and thread made of cotton have been recovered from ancient deposits in caves, cliff houses, and ruined pueblos by archeologists. But the question as to whether this cotton was derived entirely from a wild native plant has not been answered to the satisfaction of scientists. There are good reasons why the mystery may never be solved, for here is another case involving trans-Pacific travel.

Cotton given a date by botanists of 2300 B.C. has been found in Peru, and some nearly as old has been recovered in Mexico. Did cotton reach South America at an earlier time? Were Asiatic cottonseeds transported northward through Central America and Mexico to the Southwest of the Pueblos, and when and where was Asiatic cotton first crossed with native American varieties?

Remarking that fiber in cotton textiles recovered by archeologists does not give the plant geneticist all the data he needs, Driver states: *

New World domesticated cottons are crosses between domesticated Old World species and wild New World species. Each of the parent species has 13 chromosomes, while the half-breed plants have 26 chromosomes. It is difficult to date the first appearance of Old World cotton in the New World because plant geneticists must have living cells in order to count chromosomes and make other microscopic observations. Although we cannot prove that this early [South American and Mexican] cotton has 26 chromosomes, it otherwise possesses the characteristics of the half-breed barbadense plant and suggests that Asiatic cotton had found its way to the Americas by that date. Because the Old World domesticated species did the traveling, it seems to have been brought to the New World by boats.

* *Op. cit.*

It seems true as well that, in any event, Indians of the Southwest, both men and women, were making use of cotton in weaving far back in time. The anthropologist John R. Swanton * puts the matter in these words:

Cotton has been raised to a considerable extent by the Pueblos, especially the Hopi, from time immemorial.

How long that may be, however, is a matter that rests on many unresolved problems.

Nunez Cabeza de Vaca was the first European to write of cotton textiles made by Pueblos. He saw them in northwestern Mexico among Indians who had obtained them in trade from the north, that is, from the Hopi, Zuni, and other people who dwelt in large towns. In his opinion the Pueblo cotton shawls were "better than those of New Spain [Mexico]."

When in 1540 Coronado reached the Pueblo country, he found cultivated cotton growing in irrigated fields adjacent to many pueblos, and cotton garments and blankets taken by force from the Indians kept him and his suffering soldiers warm through two bitterly cold winters.

Indian women not only were skilled in making pottery, weaving baskets and garments, and dressing skins, but in many regions they displayed considerable artistry in decorating and coloring the products of these crafts. Strangely, men usually painted naturalistic figures of human beings and animals, and women almost universally confined their painting to geometric designs, and circular and straight lines. This was also true of the designs woven into baskets and cloth by women.

* *Op. cit.*

Designs were made in cloth by a method known as tie dying. Under this technique, women folded the textile at various points and tied the folds tightly with string. When it was dipped momentarily in dye, the dye did not penetrate the folded areas. Pottery also was decorated by incising the soft surface before firing.

The women were well versed in manufacturing colors and dyes. Permanent dyes were made from organic materials. Basket makers of many tribes were satisfied with natural colors, making their dyes from the red and black of bark, the white of grass stems, yellow of peeled rods and rushes, and brown of root bark. Most of the women of the Southwest used only black for designs on baskets. Northeastern women made fugitive stains from berries. Lichens, goldenseal, bloodroot, and the bark of the butternut were used by women of northern and eastern tribes. Virginia Indian women used sumac and tree bark to obtain dyes for deerskin mantles, mats, and baskets. The use of dyes required a knowledge of mordants, and various types were prepared. Southwestern women used urine. Alum, iron salt, and organic acids also were used.

The inorganic colors used by Indian women were mostly derived from iron-bearing minerals, such as ochers and other ores, and stained earths. Walter Hough * states:

These furnished various tints, as brown, red, green, blue, yellow, orange, and purple. White was derived from kaolin, limestone, and gypsum; black from graphite, powdered coal, charcoal, or soot; green and blue from copper ores and phosphate of iron. Pigments were rubbed into soft tanned skins, giving the effect of dye.

* Hodge, 1906.

The manufacture of beads was usually the work of male craftsmen, but primitive women wove them into fabrics, used them to decorate utensils and ceremonial costumes, and constructed ornaments of them. The beads were made of a great variety of mineral, vegetal, and animal materials, among them copper, hematite, quartz, serpentine, magnetite, slate, soapstone, turquoise, encrinite sections, pottery, seeds, nuts, stems, roots, shell, bone, horn, teeth, and claws.

Porcupine quill work was an ancient craft, and products ranked in beauty and colorfulness with any made by Indian women. Embroidering articles with quills was time-consuming work. Alice C. Fletcher states: *

Technical skill as well as unlimited patience was required to make even, smooth, and fine quillwork, and proficiency could be acquired only by practice and nice attention to details.

The art reached its highest development in areas in which the porcupine was most abundant, and especially among tribes that had a stable food supply and whose men were the chief providers, conditions that, as Fletcher notes, "made it possible for the women to have the leisure necessary for them to become adept in the working of quills."

The quills were softened with water, pressed flat, dried, and then sorted into lengths. The various sizes were dyed different colors.

The articles most commonly decorated with quills were those made of dressed skin, although both utensils made of bark and decorations and ornaments made of animal hair were embroidered. Quill work was done on tobacco pouches,

* Hodge, 1906.

tinder bags, cases, cradles, amulets, burden straps, arm and leg bands, tunics, shirts, leggings, moccasins, and robes. Among some tribes certain designs were used exclusively on men's garments, and others were embroidered only on clothing and ornaments worn by women. Both sexes invented designs, and a man might instruct a woman as to the figures or patterns he desired for his garments. The finished product of a woman expert in quill work was not only smooth and even but presented a glossy surface like that of straw.

Many designs were symbolic and were attributed to dreams sent by the Great Spider, who was the supreme master of the art of embroidery.

6
Adornment

The women wore a cloth around their bodies fastened by a girdle which extended below the knees, but next to the body, under this coat, they used a dressed deerskin coat, girt around the waist. The lower body of this skirt they ornamented with strips taste- fully decorated with wampum which was frequently worth from 100 to 300 guilders [$40 to $120]. They bound their hair behind in a club, about a hand long, in the form of a beaver's tail, over which they drew a square wampum-oramented cap; and when they desired to be fine they drew around the forehead a band also ornamented with wampum, which was fastened behind in a knot.

—A. van der Donck, describing Hudson River Indian women, c. 1640

It is not difficult to imagine four specks appearing on a distant rise. The sentries of the village or the pueblo give the alarm and watch them. Always the sentries are squinting into distance. Not animals this time, but men. The children are gathered. The men might be scouts for an attacking party, and the women see that the water jars are full and that food caches are covered to conceal them. The men look to their weapons. The dogs have sighted the strangers, and retreat to their hiding places with growls, or circle about nervously, barking.

The four men approach slowly, pausing now and then and giving signs. They are signs of peace, of friendship. But the village or the pueblo remains alert, on guard, ready. The four men hold up pieces of colored cloth, or furs, or painted gourds, or articles containing bits of stone that catch the sunlight and throw it out. From the village or the pueblo, several men cautiously emerge, and seeing them, the strangers sit down.

Traders.

There may be some brief talking, with words if the languages are mutually understandable, with signs if they are not. Then all go into the village or the pueblo. There are shouts and signs of welcome. The trading blankets are spread. A pipe is smoked. There is laughter and banter.

The women gather about in pleasure and excitement. There may be new things to gaze at in wonder and admiration. There may be new ideas. The mind is awakened, and the isolation, for a brief time, is interrupted.

Then the hills are empty again, and the sentries squint once more into distance.

The intertribal bartering of goods that were of special interest to women played an extremely significant part in the development of the prehistoric Indian economy, and this continued to be true long after the penetration of America by

Europeans, even, it might be said, after white men had monopolized the commerce of the Indian world. Such things as dishes, baskets, mats, bags, pottery, and other utilitarian articles, of course, comprised a large percentage of the trade directed toward women, but there were many other items that not only augmented that trade in a large degree but aroused the interest of women to a much greater extent than commonplace products. These were articles that contributed in some manner to personal adornment.

Costume was important to primitive Indian women. They were style-conscious. They sought new ways to adorn themselves; kept an eye out for innovations in jewelry, baubles, gewgaws, cosmetics, scents; strove for ideas to make themselves attractive and to stir envy in their contemporaries. Vanity was not an invention of women of another race.

Archeology and the accounts of early explorers, missionaries, and travelers make clear the influence of inter-regional exchange on Indian fashions. Indian women were no different from those of any country on earth in their desire to acquire unusual "foreign" ornaments. In every geographical region were found substances—animal, vegetable, and mineral—which were adaptable to paints, jewelry, and decoration, and which differed from substances obtainable in other regions.

Bits and pieces of materials that could be strung as beads or utilized in other forms of ornamentation serve as an example. From the far north came beads of walrus ivory. From the eastern coast came beads made from clam, oyster, quahog and periwinkle shells. From the subtropical South came beads made of wood, as well as of many kinds of oddly shaped and highly colored shells. From the Southeast and the Midwest came fresh water pearls. From the Pacific Coast came exquisite beads of dentalium, abalone, and olivella shells. From the Rocky Mountains and the northern Great Plains came beads of animal teeth, among them the highly valued milk teeth of the elk. From several regions came the claws of bears for pendants, and these were eagerly sought by tribes of the southern Great Plains and the Southwest. From the pueblos came the famous beads of turquoise which so delighted all women.

Face, hair, and body paints, especially reds of various hues, were always steady sellers. Generally these paints were mixed with animal grease and saliva. Garments of Indian women rarely had pockets, and there was always a good market for small bags and pouches of new types and decorated in some unusual manner. They were used to carry personal toilet articles, needles, thread, paint, medicines, and tobacco. Cosmetics and scents were trade staples. Concoctions made from animal fats and vegetable oils were used to beautify the hair and anoint the body. Sweet grass and scented seeds were the bases of most perfumes, although fish and whale oils were used, and some women are known to have considered skunk oil a delightful odor and to have used it profusely in their toilet.

Although Indian women of each area made use of feathers available to them, they also sought different kinds that were to be obtained only in certain regions. Ivory-billed woodpecker scalps and parrakeet skins were in great demand among the women of central tribes. Wild turkey feathers were desired by women in whose homelands this species was not found. California Indian women particularly liked the feathers of eastern woodpeckers, meadowlarks, crested quail, bluejays, and orioles. The colorful plumage of tropical birds, brought north from Mexico, was highly valued by many tribes. Feathers were good business—anywhere.

That prehistoric trade trails were long, and that innumerable products for women moved far over them, there can be no doubt. In midcontinent archeological sites artifacts have been found from both the eastern woodlands and the far western mountains, from the Atlantic Coast and the Pacific Coast. When the first voyageurs from French Canada—who, regrettably, cannot be identified with certainty—reached the Upper Missouri River country, the Dakota (Sioux) possessed dentalia shells from the Pacific and wampum from the Atlantic. Many other prehistoric women of the interior had seashell necklaces, and they owned belts, armlets, garters, and bracelets with shells woven into them—certain proof of the length of trade channels. Ohio Indian women had ornaments of obsidian and grizzly bear claws, raw products that came from the Rocky Mountains.

All peoples benefitted intellectually and improved their ways of living by exchanging products and ideas. How the economy of even a very small tribe, the Havasupai, was augmented by interregional trade is worthy of examination. Perhaps never numbering more than three hundred, the Havasupai were driven from place to place by stronger peoples, and at last vanished into one of the most remote and inaccessible parts of the Southwest, a place now known as Cataract Canyon, a branch of the Grand Canyon. There they came upon something of great value—a fine red ocher. Havasupai women were not especially good potters, and to obtain pottery and other products they needed, they offered the red ocher in trade with the Hopi. It soon became famous, for from the ocher could be made a superior grade of red paint eagerly desired by women. The Hopi traded the ocher to women of the Rio Grande pueblos and as far east as Santa Fe and Taos. The demand soared. Actually, not only did women prize it as a cosmetic, but both men and women found it durable and attractive, and wanted to use it in certain ceremonials and dances. The Havasupai enjoyed a prosperity they had never experienced. So valuable did the red ocher become that it was traded by the spoonful at an extremely high price.

The needle with an eye was unknown to prehistoric Indian women. In sewing they used awls of various lengths and fineness. Usually they were made of bone. The material being sewn was punctured, and the sinew or fiber thread was pushed through the hole. Some women of the Southwest used the sharp spine of the yucca as an awl. Wooden knitting needles were used among the Pueblos. Despite their crude and laborious method of sewing, Indian women produced work of exceptionally high character, showing their great skill in using the simple awl.

Contrary to an erroneous impression common among uninformed persons, primitive Indians of the United States region belonged in general to the wholly clothed peoples of the world. Naturally, more and heavier garments were worn in the northern regions than in the South and on the Pacific Coast. Even in the hottest weather, however, men normally wore a breechcloth. Except on rare ceremonial occasions, when nudity was mandatory, women did not appear in public without a short skirt. Numerous early narratives attest to this fact, and women's skirts, or fragments of them, have been found in many old archeological sites. Nunez Cabeza de Vaca wrote that Indian women on the Texas coastal plain (1529) covered themselves with a moss that grew on trees (Spanish moss) and noted that "damsels dress themselves in deerskin."

The Gentleman of Elvas (De Soto expedition, 1540) stated that women in the Southeast wore a skirt made of inner bark

or grass "about the body from the waist downward."
Writing of the Plains Apache (1541), Castaneda said:

the women are well made and modest. They cover their whole
body. They wear shoes and buskins made of tanned skin. The
women wear cloaks over their small under petticoats, with sleeves
gathered up at the shoulders, all of skin, and some wore something
like little sanbenitos * with a fringe, which reached halfway down
the thigh over the petticoat.

Lawson (1701) reported that Carolina Indian women wore
a "sort of flap or apron. . . . Sometimes it is deer-skin
dressed white, and pointed or slit at the bottom, like fringe."

Women of California tribes wore a short apron of dressed
skin or shredded bark. In the South and Southeast women's
breasts would be exposed in warm weather, but in most
other areas an upper garment was usually worn.

Ethnologist Walter Hough † states that a typical costume
of primitive Indian women differed chiefly from that of men

in the length of the shirt, which had short sleeves hanging loosely
over the upper arm, and in the absence of the breechcloth. Women
also wore the belt to confine the garment at the waist. Robes of
skin, woven fabrics, or of feathers were also worn, but blankets
were substituted for these later. The costume presented tribal differences in cut, color, and ornamentation. The free edges were
generally fringed. . . .

* A sanbenito was a garment pulled over the head, split at the sides, with front and
back flaps.

† *Op. cit.*

Noting that the Pueblos of the Southwest were the only people living wholly in the United States region who wore garments of cotton cloth in pre-Columbian times, Driver writes: *

Women wore a kind of dress which was nothing more than a rectangular piece of cotton cloth worn under the left arm and tied over the right shoulder. It was not sewn together or fastened at the right side except by a belt of the same material. An additional piece of cloth of about the same size may have been worn on top of the dress as a shawl. On the feet and lower half of the leg a combination moccasin and legging was worn. The sole was of buffalo hide, to which was sewn a piece of buckskin large enough to fold over the toe and instep. A strip of buckskin three or four feet long was wound around the moccasin proper and on up the leg to just below the knee, where it was tied fast.

Women of the Great Plains, the Rocky Mountains, northern woodlands, and deserts usually wore some type of footwear, but the use of them was unusual on the Pacific Coast and in the Southeast and the South. Some tribes near the Mexican boundary wore sandals. Sandals also have been found in archeological sites in Kentucky. Very few Indian women wore hats of any kind, but hats woven of basketry materials were worn by women in California and the Northwest.

Unlike costumes and ornamentation, women's hairstyles in most tribes adhered to traditional standards. They were not subject to new fashions, nor were they changed to an appreciable extent by individual fancies. Modes generally typical of different regions have been recorded.

* *Op. cit.*

Women of several of the larger tribes of central and northern California gathered their hair in two masses that fell in front of the shoulders. These usually were held together by a thong, but, as Kroeber * notes, might be held "on gala occasions by a strip of mink fur set with small woodpecker scalps." Long, free-flowing hair, sometimes banged on the forehead, seems to have been the prevailing mode in arid Southern California. Some women of the California deserts wore a coiled basketry cap. In the Northwest women allowed their hair to fall loose over shoulders and back.

Northern Great Plains women customarily divided their hair into two braids. Of the Sioux, Hassrick † states:

> Young girls who had not yet reached maturity wore their hair braids down the back tied with pendants, whereas those who had reached puberty wore their hair over the shoulder.

The Algonquian women of the Northeast dressed their hair in a thick, heavy plait which fell down the neck, and wore ornamented headbands.

Castaneda wrote that Pueblo women "gather their hair over the two ears, making a frame which looks like an old-fashioned headdress."

This mode was abandoned, however, some years after the Coronado expedition, except by the Hopi. Probably early in the seventeenth century most Pueblo women began to wear their hair in bangs falling almost to the eyebrows, cutting it just below the ears at the sides, and allowing it to grow full length in back. On reaching puberty, Hopi girls dressed

* *Op. cit.*

† *Op. cit.*

their hair in a large whorl on each side of the head. This style imitated the squash blossom, which was a symbol of fertility in their religious ceremonials.

Bartram recorded that Cherokee women did not cut their hair, but plaited it in wreaths which were fastened on the top of the head and held by broaches in a kind of topknot. The hair of women of the Wichita and other Caddoan tribes was permitted to flow over the back and shoulders. According to N. D. Mereness,* an early observer, Creek women

are very neat in smoothing and putting up their hair, it is so very long when untied that it reaches to the calves of their legs.

Writing of Carolina women, Lawson said:

The hair of their heads is made into a long roll like a horse's tail, and bound round with beads they make of the conk-shells. Others that have not this make a leather-string serve.

Painting the face was universally practiced by primitive Indian women. A vast variety of lines, figures, and designs was used. Often these decorations were symbolic, but probably just as often they reflected the whim of the wearer. A large number of colors were used, and women prided themselves on concocting an unusual tint. Hollow or filled circles might be placed on the cheeks, or two lines might be drawn between the forehead and the chin or across the upper lip to the ears. Eyes might be encircled. The women of many tribes pierced their ears and wore earrings or dangling ornaments. Some ceremonials required that certain painted fa-

* *Travels in the American Colonies.*

cial designs be worn, but on gala social occasions there might be no limit to which a woman would go to paint her face in a manner she thought would impress prominent visitors. Eyebrows were plucked to thin lines, or, in some cases, entirely removed. The women of some tribes plucked out all body hair, using wooden tweezers or clam shells.

Women of every region were tattooed to some extent. This form of adornment was not only decorative in character but was often indicative of status, religious beliefs, and tribal affiliation. In some tribes the designs were elaborate and covered large parts of the body. Among other peoples only certain parts were decorated.

Women in the Southeast had their legs, trunks, arms, and thighs tattooed. Facial tattooing was widely practiced by the women of the Pacific Coast. Some women had the entire chin, from the corners of the mouth downward, tattooed solidly except for two narrow blank lines. In other tribes women's faces were tattooed with lines extending from the ears to the chin, from the sides of the nose to the cheeks, or from the corners of the mouth to various other parts of the face. Among the most tattooed women north of Mexico were the Wichita. Many women of this tribe covered most of their bodies with elaborate decorations. Scholars have noted that the tattooing worn by the women of numerous tribes was similar to the designs painted on the pottery and woven into the baskets they made.

Fletcher states: *

Among the Kiowa, the tribal mark was a circle on the forehead of the woman. With the Omaha and some of their cognates a small

* *Bulletin 30*, Bureau of American Ethnology.

round spot on the forehead of a girl, and a four-pointed star on the back and breast, were marks of honor to signify achievements of her father or near of kin.

While black was probably used more than any other color, Nunez Cabeza de Vaca mentioned seeing women of the Gulf of Mexico area tattooed with red and blue, and other early explorers noted the use of various shades. Some designs were amazingly intricate and done with great artistry. The tattooing was done by men who were especially adept in the work. In most areas sharp flint instruments were used, but in the Southwest cactus spines served as needles.

7
Sex

I have been in the midst of those roaring lions, and savage bears, that feared neither God, nor man, nor the devil, by day and by night, alone, and in company; sleeping, all sorts together, and not one of them ever offered the least abuse or unchastity to me in word or in action.

> —Mary Rowlandson, wife of
> clergyman, a captive of the
> fierce Narraganset tribe for
> three months in 1676 *

Bad as the savages are, they never violate the chastity of any woman, their prisoners.

> General James Clinton, de-
> scribing the Iroquois,
> whom he was fighting,
> 1779. †

* *Bulletin 30*, Bureau of American Ethnology.

† *Ibid.*

At the outset of this chapter, it may be well to refute two fallacies long harbored by white people: (1) Indians had no principles governing moral conduct; (2) an Indian woman, married or unmarried, was chattel.

The source of the first myth is traceable back through all the missionaries who, since the New World's discovery, have sought to force Indians to adhere to the norms of Christian morals. It was, of course, a futile struggle, for Indians soon came to understand that men calling themselves Christians were diabolical hypocrites who turned their professed moral scruples on and off as they chose with some curious mental spigot.

All Indian peoples had moral standards, and in general, individually and collectively, adhered to them. These codes varied, often to a great extent, but that was because they had not devolved from human pedagogues but were based upon modes of life, upon environmental and economic conditions, and upon physical needs, and because they reflected upon the functions of the magic power that controlled reproduction in all living things. The roots of Indian moral laws reached into incalculable antiquity, much farther back into the vaults of time than those of tenets promulgated by biblical authors. Moreover, as Hodge states,* "such rules may be found more rigorously observed and demanding greater self-denial among savages than among civilized men."

Social customs that were universally observed by Indians negate the assumption of uninformed white persons that an Indian woman could be held in connubial bondage. In almost all primitive tribes, a wife possessed far more freedom to revise the pattern of her life than her counterpart of any Eu-

* *Handbook.*

ropean nationality. In fact, among Indians it was not only simple but much less expensive to achieve a divorce—or, more properly speaking, a separation—than it was to negotiate a marriage contract.

The procedure most commonly followed was for a man to obtain a bride by purchase, that is, by suitable gifts to her family. In some tribes gifts of equal value were exchanged between the kin of both the bride and groom. Completion of this transaction, however, did not make a young woman a chattel of her husband.

A wife who was abused, who was inadequately provided with the ordinary necessities of life, or who was otherwise unhappy could conclude her marriage simply by announcing that she was leaving.

In tribes in which a woman was the proprietress of the home and its contents, she could dismiss an unsatisfactory spouse with a demand that he vacate the premises or by resorting to the expedient of placing his personal effects outside the door. In any case, the ousted husband had no alternative but to comply with the ultimatum.

A man, of course, possessed similar marital rights. He could with no greater difficulty rid himself of a shrewish, lazy, or incompetent mate.

Children were not a problem that complicated the dissolution of a marriage; they remained with their mother or were taken in by members of her immediate family. After separating, a man and woman were free to remarry at will.

A family could request a bride price only for a daughter who had not been married. Normally an agreement on the amount to be paid was reached through discussions between the parents of both the prospective bride and groom. Not infrequently other relatives, such as uncles and aunts, and perhaps first cousins, had a voice in the decision to accept or reject an offer. The initial marriage of a daughter or son was a family matter. Indeed, among most Indian peoples it was regarded as both an economic and sexual contract between two groups of kin rather than between two individuals. In the final analysis, therefore, elders actually had more to do with the selection of a marriage partner for a young man or woman than did either of them.

While the purchase of brides was universal practice, the size and type of payments varied greatly. In some tribes a young man might obtain a wife of his choice by laboring or hunting for a specified time for her family. In other tribes it was customary to give articles of intrinsic value, such as furs, robes, ornaments, specially decorated garments, canoes, and weapons. In the East and Southeast strings of wampumpeage (which white men shortened to *wampum*) * generally figured in such transactions, as did strings or loose quantities of dentalium, olivella, and haliotis shells on the Pacific Coast. According to Kroeber,† a prominent family of the California Yurok expected to receive at least ten strings of dentalium, a headband of fifty woodpecker scalps, a piece of obsidian, a boat, and other valuables as a bride price. For a poorer girl, eight strings and a boat might be given.

Kroeber adds:

People's social status was determined not only by what they possessed, but by what had been given by their fathers for their moth-

---

* Wampum was made from shells such as the poquahaug, the periwinkle, the whelk, and the freshwater genus *Unio*. Its manufacture required patient labor and a high degree of skill.

† *Op. cit.*

ers. Men of wealth made a point of paying large sums for their brides. They thereby enhanced their own standing and insured that of their children. A young man of repute preserved the tradition of his lineage and honored the person and family of his wife in proportion as he paid liberally for her. A poor man was despised not only for his lack of substance, but for the little that he gave for the mother of his children, and for mean circumstances surrounding his own origin. A bastard was one whose birth had never been properly paid for, and he stood at the bottom of the social scale.

The payment of a bride price, states Driver,*

does not give the purchaser the right to dispose of the bride either by sale to another or by renting her out as a prostitute. Neither does it carry the right to injure or to kill her. All the husband purchases is the right to share with her the type of sexual and economic life permitted and approved by the society in which he lives.

Hewitt affirms that †

in most, if not in all, the highly organized tribes, the woman was the sole master of her own body. Her husband or lover, as the case may be, acquired marital control over her person by her own consent or by that of her family or clan elders. This respect for the person of the native women was equally shared by captive alien women.

A secret marriage or divorce was not possible in any Indian society. Regulations were without variance in requiring that every marriage and every separation had to be made

* *Op. cit.*

† *Bulletin 30*, Bureau of American Ethnology.

known to all adults of a community, and in some cases to all members of the clan or gens to which the principals in such an action belonged. As there were no written records, it was only by this means that social and moral laws, such as those establishing relationship, which among some Indian people extended beyond blood relatives into politically created divisions, could be adequately enforced. Without exception, mating between a man and woman who were consanguineously related was regarded as incest, even though the relationship was remote, a crime that could result in ostracism or other severe forms of punishment for its perpetrators.

No limits generally applicable can be delineated for either the incest taboo or exogamy, the rule that required a person to marry outside a specific social group. Most scientists are inclined to designate the incest taboo as a ban on marriage or mating between actual genetic relatives, and apply the term exogamy for the prohibition of sexual relations within larger kin groups which recognize traditional relationship. In tribes in which sibs exist (i.e., a combination of patrilineal or matrilineal groups descended from either a real or supposed ancestor), moral regulations were extreme in their application. Driver supplies a graphic example: *

The Creek Indians of Alabama and Georgia possessed about 40 sibs, 50 villages, and a population of about 18,000. Although the sibs averaged about 450 members, some were much larger than others and may have had a thousand members. Each village, on the average, was occupied by people from half a dozen different sibs. Rules of sib exogamy were extended to all of the 50 villages: for example, a man of the deer sib could not marry a woman of the same

* *Op. cit.*

118

sib even though she lived in another Creek village more than a hundred miles distant from his place of residence.

Across the country to the Southwest, a similar situation would have been found among the Navajo, where the social structure was based on matrilineal clans. To a Navajo, "relatives" meant the members of his or her clan, whether consanguineous or not, and they were of equal importance to both men and women. A young Navajo man and a young Navajo woman might have been born and reared in communities separated by hundreds of miles of deserts and mountains, and be not in the remotest degree blood relatives, but if they belonged to the same clan they were prohibited from marrying, even though they were deeply in love. The Navajo believed that their union would have been a repulsive crime and would result in their suffering insanity.

Punishment imposed upon violators of marriage taboos was less severe in some tribes than in others. According to Ernest Wallace and E. Adamson Hoebel: *

The Comanches actually had strong feelings about incest . . . but they felt no need to impose strong sanctions against it. Most men were too concerned with the maintenance of their personal prestige to mar it with such an act. And perhaps more important is the fact that Comanche supernaturals were in no sense projected images of a rewarding and punishing father. Incest was not a sin against the gods any more than it was a crime. There was no need to punish the offender in order to protect the community from supernatural wrath. The act remained an offense against good taste, nothing more.

* *The Comanches.*

119

As recorded by Lawson, the tribes of the Carolinas took a much more serious view of the matter: *

They never marry so near as a first cousin, and although there is nothing more coveted amongst them than to marry a woman of their own nation, yet when the nation consists of a very few people, so that they are all of them related to one another, then they look out for husbands and wives among strangers. For if an Indian lies with his sister, or any very near relation, his body is burnt, and his ashes thrown into the river, as unworthy to remain on earth. . . .

Troubles between newlyweds and mothers- and fathers-in-law were not a vexing problem among most Indian peoples. It was avoided by the simple expedient of keeping out of each other's way as much as possible; in some tribes it was considered a breach of manners for a bride to speak to, or even look at, her husband's parents, and generally the same ethical restriction was placed upon a groom with regard to his wife's father and mother.

Writing about the Sioux, Hassrick says: †

Young married couples might live briefly with one or the other's parents, but this was inconvenient and for any length of time unworkable, because of the avoidance taboo among parents and children-in-law. A wife might not look at or address her father-in-law, and similarly, a husband was prohibited from any familiarity with his mother-in-law. This was as difficult for a daughter-in-law residing with her husband's people as for a man living with his wife's family. As a result, a young couple was usually given a tipi

* *Op. cit.*

† *Op. cit.*

to be pitched in front of one or the other parents-in-law's lodges, where they might enjoy the proximity of their family without the embarrassingly difficult situations occasioned by the taboo.

An Apache man did not speak to his mother-in-law, and treated his wife's father with distant respect. The Navajo man studiously avoided his mother-in-law. The Lemhi Shoshoni regarded a man as insane if he spoke to his wife's mother. The avoidance taboo was lacking among the Hopi, Arikara, Zuni, Comanche, some Shoshoni, and a number of California tribes. The fact is noteworthy, however, that it was distributed from coast to coast, flourishing especially among large tribes in such widely separated regions as the Southeast, the Great Plains, the Southwest, and on the Pacific Coast.

There were few Indian societies in which premarital mating was not practiced and condoned. In the great majority of tribes, however, virginity and chastity brought material rewards and honors.

The attitudes about sex of the Indians inhabiting the Southeast were extremely liberal. Driver states that both young men and young women in this region were allowed premarital sexual experience,*

which was taken for granted and was nothing to be ashamed of or kept secret. The only restriction was that they should not violate the rules regarding incest. . . . Premarital pregnancies were fairly common, and the children were reared by the mother's family, extended family, or sib as a matter of course. . . . There was little or no stigma attached to the mother or the offspring of a premarital sexual union.

* *Op. cit.*

In his own inimitable style, Lawson presents an impressive account of sexual activity among the young Indians of North Carolina: *

The girls, at twelve or thirteen years of age, as soon as nature prompts them, freely bestow their maidenheads on some youth about the same age, continuing her favors on whom she most affects, changing her mate very often, few or none of them being constant to one, till a greater number of years has made her capable of managing domestic affairs, and she hath tried the vigor of most of the nation she belongs to.

Multiplicity of gallants never being a stain to a female's reputation, or the least hindrance of her advancement; but the more whorish, the more honorable, and they of all most coveted by those of the first rank to make a wife of. The Flos Virginis, so much coveted by the Europeans, is never valued by these savages.

The permissiveness of the southeastern peoples was in sharp contrast to moral persuasions in other regions. Unchastity was not condoned by the Cheyenne. Certain Crow rituals could be performed only by a woman who had been a virgin bride and who was known to have been faithful to her husband. In some tribes of the Northwest Coast, young women were obliged to sleep—indeed to spend most of their days and nights—in guarded rooms after their first menstruation until they were married. There was another purpose besides that of preserving chastity in this custom. Among the commercial-minded northwestern tribes, a virgin not only brought a high bride price but, if she was attractive, had a good chance of being purchased by the scion of a wealthy and socially prominent family, to the benefit of her parents, as well as herself.

* *Op. cit.*

Perhaps the most pronounced qualities of the Kansa, who were not enterprising nor overburdened with intelligence, were: (1) that they held an unbounded and indestructible pride in themselves; and (2) that they made uncommon efforts to instill high standards of morality in their young, and, to a greater extent than any other Great Plains people, guarded the chastity of their women.

A breach that was never healed, purportedly caused by sexual promiscuity, was created between two other Siouan tribes, the Missouri and the Oto. According to accounts heard by the first fur hunters and missionaries to reach the lower Missouri River region, the row occurred when the son of the Oto chief raped, or at least seduced, a young daughter of the Missouri chief. As a result of the incident, the tribe of the ardent young man was dubbed Oto, a name deriving from the word *wat'ota,* meaning "lechers." The tribe had another name for themselves, Che-wae-rae, the meaning of which is uncertain, but if they remembered it, others did not, and they were never able to escape the opprobrium fastened on them by the resentful chief of the Missouri. And so they became known to history—the lechers.

Two early travelers in the Southeast are quoted by David H. Corkran * as writing that when an unmarried man on a journey stayed overnight in a Creek village he hired a girl as a bedmate, and that before marriage Creek women had a right to act with men as they pleased. With regard to the Comanche of the high southwestern Great Plains, Wallace and Hoebel state † that

---

* *The Creek Frontier.*

† *Op. cit.*

their attitudes toward illegitimacy, which seems to have been rare, show no vindictiveness, although the feeling prevailed that every child should have a recognized father.

These authors add:

Premarital sex relations were common, but in case a child was born as a result, the father usually married the mother.

Lowie says of the Great Plains Indians: *

As in many civilized societies, there was a double standard: elders carefully watched the behavior of young women, while a young man was rather expected to philander. Feminine chastity was highly prized. . . .

A virtuous Sioux daughter brought the highest purchase price. Writing specifically of the Great Plains Sioux, Hassrick enlarges the subject: †

Premarital relations between the sexes, though by no means condoned by the family or parents, were nonetheless not uncommon. And to the young man who was successful went the commendation of his peers. Not only did this become a matter of conversation, but it was worthy to be counted as a coup upon his private, if not his public, record.

And Hassrick continues:

Virtue and chastity for women were more than mere prudery. The Sioux often discussed sex deviation and liberties in rather

---

* *Indians of the Plains.*

† *The Sioux.*

direct and ribald fashion, condemned transgressors publicly, and on occasion penalized them with social ostracism and physical disfigurement. They also set such a high standard for women that those who achieved it were accorded significant status and respect; in a sense they attained a goddess-like quality. And it is probably true that the boastful young man, confronted with the implications of this image, might well have subverted his physical and immediate ambitions to a long-term psychic and social gain.

A passage by Nunez Cabeza de Vaca gives an unforgettable account of the customs of some eastern Texas tribes: *

They cast away their daughters at birth, and cause them to be eaten by dogs. The reason of their doing this, as they state, is because all the nations of the country are their foes; and as they have unceasing war with them, if they were to marry away their daughters, they would so greatly multiply their enemies that they must be overcome and made slaves. . . . We asked why they did not themselves marry them; and they said it would be a disgustful thing to marry among relatives, and far better to kill them than to give them either to their kindred or to their foes.

When the men would marry, they buy the women of their enemies: the price paid for a wife is a bow, the best that can be got, with two arrows. . . . The marriage state continues no longer than while the parties are satisfied, and they separate for the slightest cause.

A Spanish religious, ministering in Texas two hundred years after Nunez Cabeza de Vaca was there, stated that the Karankawa

exchange or barter their wives. If one of them likes the wife of another better, he gives him his and something of value besides.

* *Op. cit.*

. . . They lend their wives to their friends . . . sell them for a horse, for gunpowder, balls, beads of glass and other things which they esteem.

It seems apparent that in many tribes mercenary reasons more than moral scruples prompted parents to attempt to preserve the chastity of their daughters. Kroeber's statement about a California people might well be applied to many in other regions: *

As a girl's property value was greatly impaired if she bore a child before marriage, and she was subject to abuse from her family and disgrace before the community, abortion was frequently attempted. . . . There is little doubt that parents guarded their girls carefully, but the latter give the impression of having been more inclined to prudence than to virtue for its own sake. Probably habits differed largely according to the rank of the family. Poor girls had much less to lose by an indiscretion.

This was an attitude, as has been noted, that was quite in contrast with that of southeastern Indians, but quite in accord with that of some Great Plains people.

When he was among the Pueblos of the Rio Grande, Castaneda (1540)

found out several things about them from one of our Indians, who had been a captive among them for a whole year. I asked him especially for the reason why the young women in that province went entirely naked, however cold it might be, and he told me that the virgins had to go around this way until they took a husband and that they covered themselves after they had known man. . . .

* *Op. cit.*

The virgins also go nude until they take husbands because they say that if they do anything wrong then it will be seen, and so they do not do it. They do not need to be ashamed because they go around as they were born.

Neither a betrothal nor a marriage was marked by a series of social festivities sponsored by the parents of the young couple. In some tribes, families and close friends might get together for a feast, and perhaps dance a bit, but such celebrations were not prolonged. There was no wedding ceremony presided over by priest or shaman, no religious observations. Among most peoples, once an agreement had been reached, and proper gifts exchanged, a bride and groom went to bed, either in their own new lodge or in quarters prepared for them by relatives. Sometimes, of course, they slipped away to a secret rendezvous, perhaps some place in which they had previously enjoyed each other before the completion of formalities.

There was one custom worthy of mention among the Pueblos. As, according to Castaneda, a virgin was obliged to go about undressed, her swain was required "to spin and weave a blanket and place it before her, who covers herself with it and becomes his wife."

If the marriage took place in the winter, which normally is bitterly cold in the high Southwest, the warmth of the blanket must have been greatly appreciated. And there was another custom, common among many tribes, that might be noted. On the first morning after a marriage, a young woman would somewhat ceremoniously carry out and empty a pot containing her husband's urine. This act was taken as an indication that she had indeed shared the conjugal couch with him, and would thence forth be a dutiful wife.

Polygyny, the form of polygamy that gives to a man the right to have two or more wives at the same time, was practiced by almost all Indian peoples.* Important exceptions were the Iroquois, some of their close neighbors, and two western Pueblo tribes, the Zuni and Hopi, all of whom were monogamists. Exclusive monogamy, as Driver explains,† was to be expected in cultures like those of the Iroquois and the western Pueblos

in which matrilineal descent and matrilocal residence were coupled with female ownership and control of agricultural land and houses, not to mention the unusual authority of women in political affairs.

Many factors, the least of which were sexual need or desire, provided reasons for practicing polygyny. A few may be cited: (1) Warfare and hunting accidents in some years decimated the male population of many tribes to the extent that a surplus of marriageable young women prevailed. (2) A wealthy man was expected to be host to many guests, and the duties related to his social activities were too great to be performed by one wife. He might well require three or four to carry out the obligations of lavish entertainments with desirable skill and efficiency. (3) In many tribes a young woman gained social status by becoming the wife of a prominent man, even though he had other wives.

Writing of primitive society in general, Lowie states: ‡

---

* The other form of polygamy, called polyandry, the practice that permits a woman to be married simultaneously to two or more men, is not known to have existed in America.

† *Op. cit.*

‡ *Op. cit.*

Another motive for taking wives lies in the universal longing for progeny. When the first wife is barren, it is thus a widespread practice for the husband to espouse a second woman in the hope of gaining issue through her. The sexual factor pure and simple is of course not to be wholly ignored . . . but everything seems to show that its influence on the development of polygyny is slight.

On the theory that it would reduce jealousy or other types of troubles that might occur in a household, the practice of marrying sisters was common. Indeed, in some tribes a man was accorded the first opportunity to marry a sister or the sisters of his wife. Only an economic factor limited plural marriages in most Indian societies. A man could take as many wives as he could properly support. Some tribes, however, restricted a man to a certain number of wives, perhaps four of five, regardless of his wealth. The Omaha were the only Siouan people to prohibit a man from having more than three wives.

Among the southeastern tribes, as Lawson notes,

some of their war captains, and great men, very often will retain three or four girls at a time for their own use, when at the same time he is so impotent and old, as to be incapable of making use of one of them, so that he seldom misses of wearing greater horns than the game he kills.

Indians were like all other people on earth in that among them there were all manner of sex deviates. One of the first missionaries among the Illinois, Father Zenobe Membre, wrote of them: *

* See Terrell, *La Salle*.

Hermaphrodites are numerous. . . . They are lewd, and even unnaturally so, having boys dressed as women, destined for infamous purposes. These boys are employed only in women's work. . . .

Nunez Cabeza de Vaca wrote of Texas Indians he did not identify by name:

I witnessed a diabolical practice; a man living with another. . . . These go habited like women. . . .

While the moral standards of the Choctaw could not be termed strict, they held sexual perverts in contempt. Hassrick states:

Of particular concern to the Sioux with regard to sex was the male transvestite whom they called *winkte*. While the *winkte* was not abhorred, he was surely feared. Here were males who, unable to compete as men in the rigorous hunting and war system, found escape by adopting the female role. Dressed as women, and following the feminine pursuits of tanning and quilling, they lived in their own tipis at the edge of the camp circle. . . .

Kroeber writes that the Mohave

call transvestites *alyha* and hold a ceremony inducting youths into this condition. They say that a boy dreams that he is an *alyha* and then can not do otherwise.

A skirt is made for him during the night by four men from twisted cords and shredded bark, and in the morning, after bathing, two women give the youth the front and back pieces of his new dress and paint his face white. After four days he is painted again and is an *alyha*. Such persons speak, laugh, smile, sit and act like women. They are lucky at gambling, say the Mohave, but die young. . . . Sometimes, but more rarely, a girl took on man's estate, among both Yuma and Mohave, and was then known as *hwami*, and might marry women. There was no ceremony to mark her new status.

Kroeber further states that the "frame of mind" which caused young men to prefer the life and dress of a woman

was not combatted, but socially recognized by the Indians of California—in fact, probably by all tribes of the continent north of Mexico.

A woman was entitled to leave her husband for just cause, but infidelity was considered a serious crime. Among most peoples an adulteress suffered extreme punishment, not excluding maiming, disfigurement, and other types of brutal treatment. In numerous tribes, among them the Miami, Illinois, Sioux, and Apache, the nose of an unfaithful wife might be cut off.

The Choctaw had a somewhat unique means of dealing with the problem. A husband might do nothing more than drive a wayward wife from his home, but he could, if he desired, take her to the public square of their village and there she could be forced to yield in public to any man who chose to have sexual intercourse with her. According to John R. Swanton,* an early French visitor who witnessed such a scene was informed that the procedure was based on the

* *Bulletin 30*, Bureau of American Ethnology.

belief that the way to teach lewd women a lesson "was to give them at once what they so constantly and eagerly pursued."

Men were not immune from punishment for the seduction of another man's wife. Penalties might be inflicted in numerous forms. In some tribes they were severe. The seducer might be required to pay a heavy fine in goods of value to the husband of his victim. He might be physically injured or even slain by the spouse and male relatives of the woman with whom he had the affair. He might be driven from his community. If he was a political leader, he might expect to be impeached.

In many tribes, wife stealing was considered as serious an offense as adultery. If a man wanted another man's wife, he could legally acquire her only after she had divorced her husband.

Hassrick states:

Retribution in the form of death was so frequent that wife-stealing and murder might almost be considered as concomitant in Sioux society.

Wife sharing was another matter. In many tribes it was considered simple hospitality, if not a duty, for a host to offer his wife—or one of his wives—as a bedmate to a distinguished guest. The exclusive proprietary claim of a husband to the favors of a spouse was universally recognized, and it could not be clouded by the temporary waiving of his marital rights, either for the purpose of gaining the goodwill of an influential visitor or as a mere gesture of friendship.

As an example, Lowie notes that

among the Crow a young man would temporarily surrender his wife to a comrade or to an older man whose supernatural powers he desired to share; indeed, such a surrender was a normal part of the transaction by which various Plains Indian tribes acquired certain ceremonial privileges.

Prostitution existed, but polygyny, the lenience of marriage laws, and the liberality of moral customs made it not only unnecessary but unprofitable. Invariably professional prostitutes were degraded women with no hope of social redemption. If they were permitted to pursue their calling by tribal fiat—disapproval was not necessarily indicative of intolerance among primitive Indians—they were looked down upon and could not enjoy legal prerogatives accorded persons who abided by more conventional rules of behavior.

In the South and Southeast unmarried young women could legitimately sell their charms for a price, but their freedom in this respect abruptly ended when they married. Such premarital activities were carefully distinguished from professional prostitution as practiced by inveterate libertines and social outcasts.

According to Lawson, young women of southeastern tribes who wished to gain rewards "by their natural parts"— he calls them "trading girls"—signified their intentions by affecting a special hair dress,

their tonsure differing from all others . . . which method is intended to prevent mistakes; for the savages of America are desirous (if possible) to keep their wives to themselves as much as those in other parts of the world. When any addresses are made to one of these trading girls, she immediately acquaints her parents therewith, and they tell the chief of it, (provided he that courts her be a stranger) the chief commonly being the principal bawd of the nation he rules over, and there seldom being any of these [casual mercenary affairs] agreed on without his consent. He likewise advises her what bargain to make.

The chief also required a percentage of whatever was paid to the girl for his wise counsel.*

Among the most primitive Indian peoples professional prostitution existed to such a small extent that it was a matter given little or no consideration. This was especially true in warrior societies, in which male casualties were normally heavy, and there was a surplus of women. Although he was writing of the Great Plains Sioux, Hassrick's words could be applied to a large number of western tribes:

In a close-knit society wherein the reputations of all women were known and ideally all were placed upon a pedestal, there was little opportunity for a man to attempt to satisfy secretly or consistently his sexual aggression without public disapproval. . . . The entire matter, however, for the Sioux, was not only unheard-of but unnecessary, for they could enjoy the complications of polygamy rather than the hollow despair of prostitution or the keeping of a mistress. Moreover, divorce was a comparatively simple method of disposing of one woman for another.

Historical narratives and government reports frequently and unjustly charge Indian women with moral degradation, recounting how they were easily available to male settlers

---

* While Lawson was a keen and undoubtedly accurate observer, it should be remembered that he was writing of Indians who had been exposed for some years to the pressures and customs of white colonists. Unquestionably military contingents, traders, and settlers, among whom there were a relatively small number of young women, sought attractive Indian girls, thereby making prostitution more profitable than was the case in prehistoric times.

and soldiers. These accounts should be cautiously considered, and the circumstances carefully analyzed. Illustrative of this admonition is the tragic plight of some six or seven thousand Navajo who were driven into a concentration camp on the Pecos River in New Mexico. The government failed to provide them with sufficient food or other necessities. Hundreds were forced to live in holes in the ground, sheltered only by pieces of discarded army tents, cowhides, and brush. Many were dying of malnutrition. Many were almost naked, and most of them were barefoot. They were suffering from pneumonia, tuberculosis, and venereal diseases. Navajo women sold themselves for food to the four hundred soldiers stationed at nearby Fort Sumner, with the result that syphilis and gonorrhea rapidly spread among both Indians and the troops.

Similar situations and conditions prevailed over a long period of time throughout the West. In each case Indian women were condemned as sluts, as whores, as devoid of human decency, in the hypocritical mouthings of corrupt politicians and in the puerile sermons of ministers and priests blinded to reality by moral bigotry. Not only the government but American society in general can take credit for forcing Indian women to sell themselves in a final desperate effort to survive, and under no moral standard whatsoever may their actions be defined as professional prostitution.

8
Cycle

The significance of a girl's entrance into womanhood was not only appreciated by all American tribes, but its importance was much exaggerated. It was believed that whatever she did or experienced then was bound to affect her entire subsequent life, and that she had exceptional power over all persons or things that came near her at that period.

—*John R. Swanton* *, *"Puberty"*

Among all the tribes of Indians north of Mexico, woman, during the catamenial period, and, among many of the tribes, during the period of gestation and parturition, was regarded as abnormal, extra-human, sacred, in the belief that her condition revealed the function of orenda *or magic power so potent that if not segregated from the ordinary haunts of men it would disturb the usual course of nature.*

—*J. N. B. Hewitt* †, *"Orenda"*

* Hodge, 1906.

† *Ibid.*

From the time of her first menses until she reached the menopause, a woman was required to separate herself during menstruation from others of the community in which she dwelt. Her temporary ostracism and the imposition of numerous restrictions on her activities were consequences of the awe inspired by the phenomena of periodicity.

Customarily her food was taken to her by old women who were believed to be immune to supernatural influences under these particular circumstances. A young woman was attended only by her mother, or if her mother was dead or unavailable, then by some close female relative.

During a woman's confinement, all men, even her father and brothers, sought to avoid any unnecessary communication with her. The fear prevailed that a violation of traditional taboos relating to menstruation—and there were many—might offend the gods and result in the infliction of seriously harmful, if not disastrous, economic reverses. While some tribes believed that the emergence of a girl into full womanhood was an event to be marked with religious rites, feasting, and dancing, the ceremonials and celebrations were seldom conducted before the menstrual period had ended.

Among sedentary people, small huts built at the edge of the town and facing away from it became the residences of married women during their periods. However, an unmarried young woman was usually secluded in some manner in the dwelling of her family. She might be required to cover her head with a blanket or piece of cloth when others were present. In any case, a man considered it perilous to look at a menstruant, and she was prohibited from looking at him. Even when passing a menstruation hut that was empty a man would make certain that his gaze was upon some other object, perhaps a distant hill, a tree, a cloud, or a star.

Environment, economy, social customs, and spiritual beliefs all were sources of taboos and rules pertaining to first menstruation, but they varied greatly from region to region and tribe to tribe. Among the Iroquois the pubescent girl was furnished with new dishes, spoons, and other utensils for her exclusive use during seclusion, while among many tribes such articles, although not new, were kept separate from all others during her period, and were washed in a special manner before being used again. Reaching puberty, a Cheyenne girl purified herself by allowing smoke from sweet grass, cedar needles, and white sage to pass over her body inside her blanket.

Girls of most Great Plains tribes were obliged to offer long prayers and to sew, chop wood, and dress skins during their seclusion. The Pueblo Indians paid the minimum of attention to puberty—a girl reaching it, as previously noted, dressed her hair in a certain mode; but other tribes of the Southwest, notably the Apache, marked the event with a public celebration that might continue for several days and nights.

Many people thought that hard labor during first menstruation would prevent a girl from becoming lazy in later life. A California girl was forbidden to touch her head or scratch her body during this time, except with a stick especially provided for the purpose, lest she suffer dire effects from her contamination.

Various dietary restrictions that reflected upon a tribe's subsistence techniques or the general economy were imposed on female pubescents. Among peoples who depended in large part on game for their food, the menstruating girls were prohibited from eating meat, the fear being that by doing so they might offend the spirits who controlled hunting. Among the coastal tribes, it was believed that their presence might be offensive to the spirits of fish and other seafood; therefore, they were prohibited from approaching rivers and the seashore. By obeying these rules, they did not endanger the good fortunes of any fisherman or hunter, thereby helping to protect the food supplies of their people.

In most tribes strict obedience to prescribed rules of behavior during first menstruation was demanded, and it was believed that deviations would have a deleterious effect on character and personality. A girl who did not work hard during this period might well turn out to be a lazy wife. If she ate too much, it was thought that she would be greedy in later life. If she talked too much she would become garrulous. If she giggled or laughed she would become too much inclined to hilarity. If she lied she would be forever an untruthful person.

According to Lowie (1954), it was believed by tribes of the Great Plains that the four days of a girl's seclusion during her first menstruation was the most likely time for her to acquire a vision,

which otherwise might be experienced at any time. On the fourth night the women of the camp went to the shelter; four of them controlling spirit power prayed for the girl, piled up the wood she had chopped, and pushed it over, whereupon each woman carried off some of it. The girl was led to her home ceremonially and was once more prayed for. A feast followed, and then the parents distributed presents among the guests.

The girl's puberty rite of the Apache was one of the most important in their culture, and probably the most elaborate of similar ceremonies conducted by any primitive tribe. It took place as soon as the relatives of the Apache girl to be honored could complete the required arrangements. According to Driver: *

They were hosts to all visitors, providing food and entertainment consisting of social dancing by both sexes, dancing by men wearing costumes similar to those of the Pueblo kachina dancers and impersonating mountain spirits, and also games and races. The dancing took place at night by firelight, and the games and races were held in the daytime.

The more serious part of the ceremony took place inside a special tipi made for the girl. She danced continually, except for occasional rest periods, until midnight, to the singing of a shaman and the shaking of his deer's foot rattle. On the fourth night, the dancing of the girl continued until dawn. When morning came the shaman painted the girl's face red, then made a dry "painting" of the sun on his palm with pollen and other pigments, pressed this on the girl's head, and finally painted her arms and legs white. As all the guests filed past, the shaman marked them, in turn, with the same pigments. The girl then raced to the east with children . . . and the ceremony ended.

In spite of the taboos and the restrictions to which she was obliged to adhere, for a married woman the menstrual period provided a few days during which she could enjoy relief from routine and arduous obligations. She was in a sense an "untouchable," but not in a manner detrimental to her own well-being. She was free to relax and rest and to occupy herself in her days and nights of isolation with whatever pastime she favored. She might weave a basket, make a piece of pottery, dress a skin, or sew and embroider, or she might do nothing more than gaze into the distance and contemplate the

* *Op. cit.*

natural and spiritual phenomena of her world as she saw them in reality or in her imagination. She had no cooking to do, except, perhaps, to prepare a dish for herself, for no man in his right mind would think of eating food prepared by a woman undergoing her monthly affliction. Indeed, no man would permit her to touch, or even look upon, such valued possessions as his hunting weapons, his fishing paraphernalia, and his sacred totemic objects. She was in every respect "bad medicine."

Virgil J. Vogel states: *

Indians had several remedies to overcome delayed menstruation, to control profuse menstruation, or to relieve pain.

He cites two examples from widely separated regions:

During their period Arikara [Upper Missouri River] women took an infusion of the big wild sage (*Artemisia gnaphalodes*) or the roots of the little wild sage (*Artemisia frigida*), a bitter tonic considered useful as an aid to the physiologic functions. For sanitary napkins, these women washed and cut into suitable pieces the soft and pliable buffalo-skin smoke flaps from their lodges. The Rappahannocks [Northeast] relieved menstrual pain with a tea of fresh or dried pennyroyal (*Hedeoma pulegioides*), or a tea made of split twigs of the spicebrush (*Benzoin aestivale*). The last was also used to correct delayed menses.

Lawson recorded that when menstruating, women of the Southeast

have a small string around the waist, to which another is tied and comes between their legs, where always is a wad of moss. . . .

* *American Indian Medicine.*

As among people of other races, Indian girls of low and hot regions began to menstruate between the ages of eleven and thirteen, while normally the period of puberty was a year or two later in high and cold parts of the country. Marriage did not necessarily take place, however, within a short time after a girl had achieved full womanhood. It was not prohibited, but consummation might be delayed for various reasons for a year or two, and even longer in some tribes. Bride price, social customs, clan relationship, parental objections, and personal choice were factors that might cause delays. Nevertheless, most Indian girls were married by the age of sixteen. According to the noted anthropologist Ales Hrdlicka, there were few Indian girls older than eighteen who were unmarried.

Lawson stated that girls of the Southeast

marry very young; some at thirteen or fourteen; and she that stays till twenty is reckoned a stale maid, which is a very indifferent character in that warm country. The women are very fruitful, most houses being full of little ones.

A contrary situation prevailed among the Comanche; Wallace and Hoebel noted: *

Comanche women were not very prolific, and death of the mother at childbirth was not uncommon. The average birth rate seems scarcely to have exceeded two children to each woman, and it was a rare case when there were more than three or four born to one woman. Births were far apart, and the newborn were usually small. Many women were barren.

* *Op. cit.*

Numerous scientific studies, among them those of Kroeber, Engelmann, and Hrdlicka, indicate that among the vast majority of Indian peoples a woman did not lie prone while giving birth, but remained on her knees. She usually held onto a woman attending her, or grasped a rope, strap, or post.

Wallace and Hoebel state that for Comanche women,

one or more stakes about four feet long were driven into the ground by the bed for the patient to grasp as an aid to delivery.

All tribes had remedies for inducing contractions and relieving labor pains, and the effectiveness of some has been long acknowledged by white physicians. George J. Engelmann wrote in 1883: *

Although constantly practiced by primitive peoples for thousands of years, these methods have been recently rediscovered by learned men, clothed in scientific principle, and given to the world as new.

Vogel † quotes Engelmann as saying, in reference to the third stage of labor, that the

untutored, simple-minded savage, although crude in the methods he pursues, obeys a correct, even if we should term it an animal, instinct, and approximates more closely to the techniques of science today . . . than does that of the semi-civilized, or of the ignorant of the enlightened communities of the present. Instinct has

* *Labor Among Primitive Peoples.*

† *Op. cit.*

taught these peoples the necessity of expelling the placenta, and they attain this object by the correct means. . . .

Vogel cites Josselyn's assertion that Indian wives

have the easiest labours of any women in the world. . . . They are delivered in a trice, not so much as groaning for it.

Lawson had something to say on the matter: *

The savage women of America have very easy travail with their children. . . . they have midwives amongst them . . . and some of these midwives are very knowing in several medicines, which certainly expedite, and make easy births. Besides, they are unacquainted with those severe pains which follow the birth in our European women. Their remedies are a great cause of this easiness. . . . the Indian women will run up and down the same day, without any sign of pain or sickness; yet they look very meager and thin.

Thus the men's point of view, and perhaps it should be remarked that opinions of women in labor are not to be found in the accounts. Medicine or no medicine, labor was painful, and the high rate of deaths during childbirth and the high infant mortality among primitive peoples attests to the fact that delivery was not as easy as it was judged to be by some male commentators. Protracted labor, malposition of the fetus, hemorrhages, blood clots, and other afflictions associated with births were not unknown, yet there is evidence to show that much of the time midwives and medicine men successfully combatted these difficulties with potions, man-

* *Op. cit.*

ual methods of manipulation, and other forms of treatment.

In spite of the many statements by early observers that Indian women possessed oral contraceptives, European and American physicians long contended that no such means of avoiding pregnancy existed. How wrong they were, of course, is now known. Moreover, the spacing of children practiced by the women of many tribes indicated that they used medicines to induce temporary sterility.

States Vogel:

Indian herbs were finally subjected to laboratory tests in the search for an effective oral means of controlling fertility, and some of them were found to be effective. Just as America was considered to be undiscovered before the white men found it, so the Indian drugs were unreal or of no account until white men discovered them. This is one example among many of the ethnocentric attitude which has hurt the white men more than the Indian by delaying scientific inquiry into aboriginal herbal knowledge.

Abortions were not uncommon among the women of many tribes, although destruction of a fetus was considered a crime by some peoples. Both herbal preparations and external physical methods are known to have been used.

Hassrick tells this story of the Sioux: *

Big Crow, a man who had dreamt of both the Buffalo and the Elk, gave girls medicine that would stop them from giving birth, but they could never have babies afterward. Roan Horse's sister and a friend once ate some of his medicine just for fun. But Big Crow, whose medicine they stole, would not withdraw the power because he was angry. So neither girl ever had any children.

* *Op. cit.*

Among New England Indians there were old squaws who could be engaged to perform an abortion, and it was reported that the profession was uncommonly lucrative. Among at least one tribe of the western mountains abortions were caused by beating a woman's abdomen with rocks, but other western tribes employed less crude methods. Women resorted to abortion for various reasons, among them fear of losing social status by giving birth to an illegitimate child, inability to provide for a larger family, or simply to escape responsibility. Among some tribes of the South birth control of any type was considered a criminal practice, but, according to Lawson, unmarried Carolina girls

have an art to destroy the conception, and she that brings a child in this station is accounted a fool. . . .

Not a few primitive peoples held an abiding fear of twins, believing them to be unnatural, and, therefore, an ill omen. In some tribes, notably in California, when twins of opposite sexes were born, the girl was smothered; in others both twins were killed; and putting the mother of twins to death was not unknown.

Writing of the Sioux, Hassrick states:

When twins were born, it was fortuitous if they both lived. It was believed that they had argued over which would be born first. The strongest of the two always won the right to be the eldest, but the other, being weaker, pouted after birth, was generally sickly, and frequently died. Hence, twins who lived were thought to be mysterious. . . .

It was a universal custom to deny life to a deformed baby, and in some tribes if a woman died during childbirth the infant, living or dead, was buried with her.

In almost all tribes of which there are reliable records, some type of ceremony was connected with the umbilical cord. It might be preserved in a small pouch especially made for the purpose. It might be wrapped and attached to the child and worn for some months, or even in a dried state for several years. It might be kept by the mother in some container, or the father might retain it, believing that it was blessed with some magic power.

Among the powerful Yurok of California, writes Kroeber,*

The umbilical cord is severed with a piece of quartz clamped inside a split stick, and carefully preserved in the house for about a year. When the child is about to be weaned the father takes the shred on a ridge, splits a living fir, inserts the little piece of preciousness, and binds the sapling together again.

Without exception, newborn babies were treated with unlimited loving care, and no effort was spared to prevent or combat illnesses that commonly struck in the first hours or days following birth. Babies were bathed in water in which herbs and plants known to have medicinal values had been boiled. They were anointed with oils and powdered. They were wrapped in moss, shredded plants, or bundles of soft animal hair. If a mother's milk was insufficient, remedies known to be effective in increasing the flow were given to her, and other nursing mothers acted in her place until she was cured of the deficiency. Artificial baby foods are not a modern invention. Primitive Indian women knew how to prepare formulas that were nourishing, using broth made

* *Op. cit.*

from buffalo or deer meat, mashed corn, and other ingredients.

Yet, as previously noted, infant mortality was high among primitive peoples. But it was not attributable in an excessive extent to neglect. Quite the reverse was true. Cold, heat, pestilence, malnutrition, warfare, the furies of the elements, indeed, common hardships, took a heavy toll of small bodies incapable of defending themselves against the burdens of the aboriginal way of life into which they had been born.

Although they were the same for both men and women, mortuary customs varied among tribes to a considerable extent. An Iroquois woman would be interred in a sitting position in a round hole in the ground and the grave would be covered with timber and earth. The corpse of a woman of the Southeast would be wrapped in rush or cane matting, placed in a reed coffin, and buried in a grave lined with bark and covered with logs or wooden slabs. Among some tribes of the Southwest, a woman's body was laid to rest in a sepulcher lined with stone slabs.

The Creeks of the South generally wrapped a woman's body in a blanket and placed it in a sitting posture in a circular pit, the legs bent under and tied together. Scaffold and tree burials were practiced in the northern woodlands and on the Great Plains. In the Northwest some tribes interred women in small wooden mortuary houses, some of which were elevated on posts. The many tribes of California were about evenly divided between cremation and interment. The ancient inhabitants of southern Arizona preserved the ashes of cremated bodies in urns. Most tribes maintained sacred burial grounds. Among not a few people, bodies were disinterred at certain intervals, and the skeletons were reburied in mass graves. A common custom was to bury with a woman some personal articles she had prized.

While still residing in their ancestral southern homeland, the Choctaw performed a burial rite that was seldom found, even partially, in the ceremonies of other tribes. It is best described as "bone-picking."

The Choctaw believed that the spirit of the deceased lingered near the remains for some days after death. The body of a dead person was wrapped in skins or bark and placed on a scaffold near his or her former home; beside the corpse, according to Angie Debo: *

were placed food and drink, a change of clothing, and favorite utensils and ornaments which would be needed by the spirit in its long journey to the other world. A dog was killed to provide the deceased with a companion.

There were among the Choctaw professional male and female bone-pickers who were distinctively tattooed and who allowed their fingernails to grow long. Debo relates that a body remained upon a scaffold for a fixed period, varying in length from one to six months, and during this time the

relatives frequently resorted to the foot of the platform to wail and mourn, although in warm weather the stench from the decomposing body became so intolerable that the women sometimes fainted. . . .

Swanton † stated that the Choctaw also followed the

custom of setting up poles around the new graves, on which they hung hoops, wreaths, etc., to aid the spirit in its ascent.

* *Rise and Fall of the Choctaw Republic.*

† Hodge, 1906.

And Debo adds that when the body

had remained upon the scaffold the specified time, a bone-picker was summoned, and all the relatives and friends were invited for the last rites. These mourners surrounded the scaffold, wailing and weeping, while the grisley undertaker ascended the platform, and with his [or her] long fingernails thoroughly cleansed the bones of the putrefied flesh. The bones were then passed down to the waiting relatives, the skull was painted with vermillion, and they were carefully placed in a coffin. . . . The flesh was left on the platform, which was set on fire; or it was carried away and buried. The hamper of bones was borne with much ceremonial wailing to the village bone house. . . . There it was placed in a row with other coffins, and the mourners all returned to the house [of the dead person's family], where all participated in a feast over which the bone-picker presided (without washing his hands, as shocked white observers were wont to state).

The famed missionary-explorer Father de Smet learned of a traditional Crow mourning custom while passing through the Yellowstone River region, in the present state of Montana, in the fall of 1840. In his invaluable journal he recorded that he and the small group of Flathead Indians escorting him suddenly came upon a heap of stones "piled up on a little eminence. . . . these stones were covered with freshly shed blood." *

De Smet quoted the chief scout of the Flatheads as telling him through their interpreter:

I think I can explain to you what we see before us. . . . we are upon one of the Crows' battlefields; their nation will have met some

* Terrell, *Black Robe*.

great loss here. This heap of stones has been raised to the memory of the warriors who had fallen. . . . Here, the mothers, wives, sisters, daughters of the dead—you see their traces—have come to weep over their graves. It is their custom to tear their faces, cut their arms and legs and shed their blood upon these stones.

A few years after the Civil War, Stephen Powers, a young journalist and amateur ethnologist, spent considerable time in the mountainous wilderness of northern California. Although in the two previous decades American miners and settlers had wantonly murdered thousands of Indian men, women, and children, the ancient culture of some of the more remote tribes had not yet been completely destroyed. Powers, a bold adventurer, a keen observer, and possessed of the ability to portray vividly and dramatically what he saw, was not too late to witness ceremonials of great antiquity. He wrote a book of inestimable anthropological value, a classic of western Americana. Of special interest here is his account of a "dance for the dead," conducted by the Yokut tribe for a woman who had recently died. She had been a sister of a prominent man named Kolómusnim, and the spectacle was held at night in a place known to prospectors as Coarse Gold Gulch. Powers wrote: *

For the last hour or so the mourners and their more intimate friends and sympathizers, mostly women, had been collecting . . . and preparing their offerings. Occasionally a long, solitary wail came up, trembling on the cold night wind. At the close of the third proclamation they began a death-dance, and the mourners crowded promiscuously in a great, open booth, and held aloft in their hands or on their heads, as they danced, the articles they intended to offer to the memory of the departed.

* *Tribes of California.*

It was a splendid exhibition of barbaric gew-gaws. Glittering necklaces of *Haliotis* and other rare marine shells; bits of tapestry; baskets of the finest workmanship, on which they had toiled for months, perhaps for years, circled and furred with hundreds of little quail-plumes, bespangled, scalloped, festooned, and embroidered with beadery until there was scarcely place for the handling. . . .

[Kolómusnim held a] pretty plume of metallic-glistening ravens' feathers in his hand.

Powers thought the most remarkable offering was carried by a woman,

a great plume, nearly six feet long, shaped like a parasol slightly opened, mostly of ravens' feathers, but containing rare and brilliant plumage from many birds of the forest, topped with a smaller plume or kind of coronet, and lavishly bedecked through all its length with bulbs, shell-clusters, circlets of feathers, dangling festoons—a magnificent bauble, towering far above all . . . contrasting so strangely with the tattered and howling savages over whom it gorgeously swayed and flaunted.

The beholding of all these things, some of which had belonged to the departed, and the strong contagion of human sorrow, wrought the Indians into a frenzy. Wildly they leaped and wailed; some flung themselves upon the earth and beat their breasts. There were constant exhortations of grief. . . . Kolómusnim, a savage of majestic presence . . . was so broken with grief that his few sobbing words moved the listeners, like a funeral knell. Beholding now and then a special friend in the circle, he would run and fall upon his knees before him, bow down his head to the earth, and give way to uncontrollable sorrow. Others of the mourners would do the same, presenting to the friend's gaze the object which had belonged to the lamented woman. The friend, if a man, would pour forth long condolences; if a woman, she would receive the mourner's head in her hands, tenderly stroke down her hair, and unite her tears and lamentations with hers.

About one o'clock in the morning, upon some prearranged signal, women thronged forward

and quickly formed a ring close around the fire—a single circle of maidens, facing inward. The whole multitude of the populous camp crowded about them in confusion, jostling and struggling. A choir of male singers took their position hard by and commenced the death song. . . .

At the same instant the young women began their frightful dance, which consisted of two leaps on each foot alternately, causing the body to rock to and fro; and either hand was thrust out with the swaying, as if the offering it held were about to be consigned to the flames, while the breath was forced out with violence between the teeth, in regular cadence, with a harsh and grinding sound of *heh!* The blaze of the sacred fire flamed redly out between the bodies of the dancers, swaying in accord, while the disheveled locks of the leaping hags wildly snapping in the night wind, the blood-curdling rasp of their breath in concert, and the frightful ululations and writhings of the mourners conspired to produce a terrible effect. At the sight of this weird, awful, and lurid spectacle, which was swung into motion so suddenly, I felt all the blood creep and tingle in my veins, and my eyes moisten with the tears of a nameless awe and terror. We were beholding now, at last, the great dance for the dead.

All the remainder of that frenzied night . . . those women leaped in the maddening dance, through smoke, and choking dust, and darkness, and glaring light, and cold, and heat, amid the unceasing wail of the multitude, not knowing or heeding aught else on earth. Once in five or ten minutes, when the choir completed a chorus, there was a pause of a few seconds; but no one moved from her place for a moment. What wonder that only the strongest young maidens were chosen for the duty! What wonder that the men avoided this terrible ordeal!

About four o'clock, wearied, dinned and benumbed with the

cold of the mountains, I crept away to a friendly blanket and sought to sleep. But it was in vain, for still through the night-air were borne up to my ears the far-off crooning, the ululations, and that slow-pulsing horrid *heh!* of the leaping witches, with all the distant voices, each more distinct than when heard nearer, of the mourning camp.

The morning star drew itself far up into the blue reaches of heaven, blinking in the cold, dry California air, and still all the mournful riot of that Walpurgis Night went on.

Then slowly there was drawn over everything a soft curtain of oblivion; the distant voices blended into one undistinguishable murmur, then died away and were still; the mourning was ended. . . .

9
Children

Those people love their offspring the most of any in the world, and treat them with the greatest mildness.

— *Nunez Cabeza de Vaca, describing Texas Indians, 1528*

The words above might be applied to all Indian peoples.

A vast amount of material exists to show that affection, kindness, and attention were bestowed in illimitable measure on Indian children.

There was seldom neglect, for if a child's parents died of illness or were lost in warfare, relatives quickly filled the empty places. Moreover, under the social structures of primitive tribes, no person could be without some type of kinship. In the absence of close consanguineous ties, it was reckoned by clan, sib, or extended family affiliation.

Except under the most unusual circumstances, physical punishment, even in mild form, was not inflicted. Equally as rare were loud scolding and severe reprimands. The burdens of adversities fell last upon the children. In times of danger they were the first to be provided with available protection. In times of want they were the first to be fed. Always the welfare of the little ones preceded other considerations.

The statements of scholars and early observers amply demonstrate that the methods Indians employed in governing and training their children were marked not only by extraordinary patience and tolerance but were to a considerable extent psychological, and were applied, as a case might require, to curb or to encourage manifested behavorial tendencies.

The Comanche, say Wallace and Hoebel,* "did not whip or otherwise bodily punish their children but directed them by persuasion and object lessons."

Parents understood that

parental dominance breeds resentment, and so, like most American Indians, when forceful discipline was called for, they turned the job over to a relative outside of the immediate conjugal family or to an imaginary bogeyman.†

A child soon learned, continue Wallace and Hoebel,

that he could not have his whims gratified by crying. He was told to do, or warned to refrain from doing, certain things, not because they were right or wrong, but because they were to his advantage or disadvantage. He was taught that he would benefit by acting in

* *The Comanches.*

† *Ibid.*

a certain way. His pride and ambition were appealed to, and worthy examples among living men in the tribe were pointed out for emulation. Of abstract principles of right or wrong, as we understand them, the Comanches knew little or nothing. The approach to life was pragmatic.

The child was, in fact, writes Mooney,*

the strongest bond of family life under a system which allowed polygamy and easy separation. Both parents alike were entirely devoted to their children, and bestowed upon them the fullest expression of affection and solicitude. The relation of parent to child brings out all the highest traits of Indian character.

Speaking of the Sioux, Hassrick states: †

Scaring a child into obedience was never flagrantly practiced, but the use of culture frighteners such as the owl . . . were commonly employed. Children who could not overcome bed-wetting were threatened by being told they would be féd mice. This was considered to be a very effective remedy.

Physical violence was never resorted to in child discipline.

Both parents assumed an active interest in the child's development, but the father's duties as hunter and warrior forced the mother to oversee and mind the children to a greater extent. . . . Both she and the father, however, inculcated family pride and respect for elders, and instilled the code of ethics and rules of etiquette through their constant preaching.

The obedience of Indian children was remarked upon by numerous white men who were among primitive tribes, but

* *Bulletin 30*, Bureau of American Ethnology.

† *The Sioux.*

in their statements are not to be found implications that either boys or girls lacked spirit or appeared cowed, or that they did not play and romp with normal enthusiasm and joyous laughter.

In 1701 Lawson wrote that Carolina

children of both sexes are very docile and learn anything with a great deal of ease. . . . Mothers never want plenty of milk, yet I never saw an Indian woman with very large breasts; neither does the youngest wife ever fail of proving so good a nurse as to bring her child up free from the rickets and disasters that proceed from the teeth, with many other distempers which attack our infants in England, and other parts of Europe.

Lawson noted that Indian women of Carolina

let their children suck till they are well grown, unless they prove big with child sooner. After delivery they absent the company of a man for forty days.

Regarding treatment Lawson stated that

I never saw a scold amongst them, and to their children they are extraordinary tender and indulgent. . . .

Abstinence from intercourse for some time after childbirth was customarily practiced by all tribes from which information on the subject has been obtained. The period greatly varied; the forty days of which Lawson speaks are unusually short, for among most peoples it was longer, and ranged from several months to a year or even, in some instances, to eighteen months or two years.

The spacing of pregnancies had no association with spiritual beliefs, but was followed for purely practical reasons. It was believed that breast feeding provided nourishment more beneficial than any other kind in the first stage of life. Weaning was rarely attempted before the age of two years, and usually not before the age of three or four.

In the case of the Sioux, as cited by Hassrick,

children usually were weaned when they reached three years, though this might vary in either direction by as much as a year. It was believed that a child should be nursed as long as possible, for this ensured good health. Supplementary feeding, however, might begin as early as one year. Meat, pre-masticated by the mother or older sisters and dipped in soup, was given the child to suck.

A husband was expected to abstain from sexual intercourse with his wife so that lactation would not halt. This might be as long as from three to four years for it was important not to jeopardize the healthy development of the child.

Speaking in general of Indians, Hrdlicka states: *

Maternal love is strong, especially during the earlier years of the child. Sexual love is rather simply organic, not of so intellectual an order as among whites; but this seems to be largely the result of views and customs governing sex relations and marriage.

Traveling through Texas in 1535, Nunez Cabeza de Vaca and his three companions encountered tribes in which men followed the custom

from the time in which their wives find themselves pregnant of not sleeping with them until two years after they have given birth.

* Hodge, 1906.

The children are suckled until the age of twelve years [?], when they are old enough to get support for themselves. We asked why they reared them in this manner; and they said because of the great poverty of the land, it happened many times, as we witnessed, that they were two or three days without eating, sometimes four, and consequently, in seasons of scarcity, the children were allowed to suckle, that they might not famish; otherwise those who lived would be delicate, having little strength.

All Indians provided educational toys for their children. Little bows and arrows were made by fathers for their sons. They played hunting and war games, and were told tales of great feats performed by legendary warriors. Mothers provided little girls with dolls and small cradle boards and tiny dishes, and the tots played at cooking and caring for their babies and performing other duties of women. When a girl was five or six, she would be taken by her mother to gather plants and berries and nuts. Usually mothers and their children went in a group to perform these essential tasks.

Only when very small was a child confined most of the time in a cradleboard. This was a safety precaution. A cradleboard could be placed to one side or suspended from a pole, and the baby was out of danger. It also allowed the baby to be easily transported. Among most tribes, when circumstances permitted, a small tot was allowed to romp about the tipi or outside with other children.

Lowie writes: *

While a Pueblo woman carried her child's cradle in her arms, a Plains Indian mother transported it on her back by means of a buckskin band across her chest and upper arms. On the march the

* *Op. cit.*

baby in its cradle might be put into a willow basket attached to a travois. . . . The Kiowa, Comanche, and Dakota put the baby into a skin pocket elaborately beaded and attached to a "lattice" frame of two tapering flat sticks converging toward the bottom. The Arapaho placed a U-shaped framework inside the buckskin cover for the child, the U being made by bending a willow branch and fixing the position by means of a transverse stick. The Blackfoot, Kutenai, Crow, Nez Perce, Shoshone, and Ute substitute for this type of frame was a board U-shaped at the top and tapering toward the bottom. . . . In many cases the cradle was profusely ornamented.

The skin-covered cradleboard was predominate among the buffalo-hunting tribes. The hide, with the hair on, was rolled to hold the infant. When these cradles were composed only of hide they were seldom decorated.

Among some Great Plains tribes, cradles made of dressed skins were lashed to a lattice of flat sticks, and Otis T. Mason,* an authority on cradles, thought that

in these are to be seen the perfection of this device. The infant, wrapped in furs, was entirely encased. Over the face was bent a flat bow adorned with pendants or amulets and covered, in the best examples, with a costly hood. The whole upper surface of the hide was a field of beadwork, quillwork, or other decoration, in which symbolic and heraldic devices were wrought. . . . Among some tribes the upper ends of the frame projected upward and were decorated.

The Algonquian, Iroquois, and other peoples of the East used a thin, rectangular board in cradles. They were fre-

* *Bulletin 30*, Bureau of American Ethnology.

quently carved and gorgeously painted, and had a projecting footrest.

The Pawnee made a cradleboard of wood taken from the
heart of a tree which had been ceremoniously selected for the
purpose. Preservation of the tree's heart was made in the
belief that without this magic influence the infant would not
survive. A wildcat skin was used for a cover, the spots on it
symbolizing the stars. The cradle bow represented the sky,
and a crooked furrow cut on it signified lightning, the power
of which was typified by a cluster of arrows.

In the coastal regions of California and Oregon, cradles
were almost like little chairs. The child's feet were free, and
it sat in the basket. Mothers lavished their skill on these sitting cradles, decorating them and adorning them with all
manner of trinkets, providing sun shades and the softest
bedding available.

Two carriers were made for Apache babies, a temporary
one at the time of the baby's birth and a permanent one three
months or so afterward. To make the baby comfortable a soft
bedding of shredded bark or crumpled grass was placed on
the face of the carrier. Over this bedding was laid the
tanned, spotted hide of a fawn, the hair side up, or at times
the skins of cottontail rabbits. The baby was then placed on
this, and between its legs for a diaper was put soft, shredded
bark. Another fawn skin, hair side in, was laid over it, the
edges tucked in about the baby's body and up under its feet.
It was then laced into the carrier with a strip of buckskin.

Grenville Goodwin * recorded that the head of an Apache
baby was pillowed on Abert squirrel or sometimes a piece of
beaver fur. The latter was thought to keep all sickness from

* See bibliography.

the baby, for "Beaver had power." Various things designed either to amuse the baby or to act as charms were attached to the hood. Sometimes the beard from the breast of a turkey cock was fastened where the baby could watch it swinging back and forth, or the turkey beard, the tail of an Abert squirrel, and the striped cones from the western yellow pine (thrown to the ground by these squirrels) were tied together and hung inside of the carrier, near the baby's head. The squirrel tail was to make a baby a good climber, the striped pine cones to keep it from being injured in falling from trees, and the turkey beard merely for ornament. If the claw of a bear could be obtained, it might also be tied on the inside of the wooden part of the hood. This kept all sickness away because "Bear had great power." Pieces of an oriole's nest were likewise used to bring good luck, as it was believed they were composed of every known species of tree. Other objects tied to the hood were stone arrowpoints and bits of prehistoric shell beads or bracelets, all safeguards against disease or accident.

As previously stated, in many tribes navel cords were preserved in various ways and the disposal of them was marked with some type of ceremony. Among the Apache, when the navel cord dried up and dropped from the newborn baby, it was wrapped in downy turkey feathers or a small piece of buckskin and tied to the wooden part of the cradle hood, inside and to either the right or left of the baby's head. Later, the mother unwrapped it, and, if the baby was a boy, buried it in a deer track to make him a good hunter. If the baby was a girl, the little dried piece of navel cord might be placed in a mescal plant or buried in a cornfield, so that when the girl grew up she would work hard at making mescal and producing crops.

When an Apache baby's first temporary carrier was discarded for the permanent one, it was hung on a tree, and was not supposed to be touched. Before it rotted and fell apart, the baby would be old enough for the mother to show it to him or her in the tree. She would tell the child: "Here is what you were in when you were a baby."

If a baby had been sick in its permanent carrier, the carrier would be abandoned, but if the infant had been exceptionally well in it, the permanent carrier would be kept and used for as many as two succeeding babies.

A permanent carrier that was no longer to be used was also put away in a tree. The mother always took the carrier to the east side of a young tree. The child in it was removed, and the carrier was hung high in the east side of the tree. If the child was a boy, any strong type of tree might be used, but usually if the child was a girl some species of food-bearing tree, such as pinon, would be selected, so that she would gather much wild plant food in later years. As the mother hung the carrier in the tree, she would say to it: "Here is the baby carrier. I put this on you, young and still growing. I want my child to grow up as you do." *

A special type of little buckskin shirt was worn by Apache infants after they had outgrown their permanent carriers. This had a long, loose belt of buckskin attached about the waist and hanging down the back, by which the child could be lifted and slung over the shoulder of the mother.

In all tribes the responsibility of caring for young children seldom rested upon the mother alone. These tasks were considered to be family obligations, and grandmothers, aunts, and older sisters assisted in the work.

* Goodwin.

All girls, as soon as they were old enough and considered responsible—perhaps as early as seven years of age—were assigned regular household duties. Minding a younger brother or sister and seeing that he or she was properly fed might be an individual responsibility of a girl nine or ten. At this age girls also helped with the cooking, gathered wood, and carried water from a stream to the tipi. Boys had more freedom from household chores, for these were looked upon as essentially women's work; moreover, it was important that boys be trained as early as possible in the manly professions of shooting, hunting, and warfare. Thus, boys old enough spent much of their time with their fathers, uncles, older brothers, or other men, learning to be warriors and meat providers.

Primitive Indian children had tops, skates made of the rib bones of large animals, darts, hummers, and balls, and such games as shinny and hunt-the-button were favorites. Wherever it was possible, youngsters of both sexes spent hours in the water each day in warm weather. Little girls frequently dressed puppies and carried them on their backs like babies, in imitation of their mothers.

Mooney * states that

as aggressiveness and the idea of individual ownership were less strong with the Indian than with whites, so quarrels were less frequent among Indian children and fighting was almost unknown. Everything was shared alike among the circle of Indian playmates. The Indian child had to learn his language as all others learned theirs, lisping words and confusing grammatical distinctions at first, but with the precocity incident to a wild free life, the Indian

* *Op. cit.*

child usually acquired correct expression at an earlier age than the average white child.

At the time they neared, or possibly had reached, adulthood, girls were not subjected to the physical ordeals of rituals that boys were required to endure. An exception to this custom, however, was recorded by Lawson in his narrative (1701–1705) about the Siouan tribes of the Southeast, for he claimed that both girls and boys were subjected to terrifying initiation ceremonies.

In his vivid account of this Siouan practice, he wrote in part:

once a year, at farthest, once in two years, these people take up so many of their young men and *husquenaugh* them,* which is to make them obedient and respectful to their superiors, and as they say, is the same to them as it is to us to send out children to school, to be taught good breeding and letters.

This house of correction is a large, strong cabin, made on purpose for the reception of the young men and boys that have not passed the graduation already; and it is always at Christmas that they *husquenaugh* their youth, which is by bringing them into this house and keeping them dark all the time, where they more than half starve them.

Besides, they give them pellitory bark, and several intoxicating plants, that make them go raving mad as ever were any people in the world, and you may hear them make the most dismal and hellish cries and howlings that ever human creatures expressed; all of which continues about five or six weeks, and the little meat they eat is the nastiest, loathsome stuff, and mixed with all manner of

---

* The word is *huskanaw*, and is from the Algonquian language. It has come down in various spellings, and has been used by early writers as a noun, verb, and adjective. Thomas Jefferson wrote: "He has the air of being huskanoyed. . . ."

filth it is possible to get. After the time is expired, they are brought out of the cabin. . . .

Now when they first come out, they are as poor as ever any creatures were; for you must know that several die under the diabolical purgation. Moreover, they either really are, or pretend to be dumb, and do not speak for several days . . . and look so ghastly, and are so changed that it is next to an impossibility to know them again, although you were ever so well acquainted with them before.

They play this prank with girls as well as boys, and I believe it is a miserable thing they endure, because I have known several of them to run away at that time to avoid it.

Now the savages say if it were not for this, they could not keep their youth in subjection, besides that it hardens them ever after . . . to all manner of hardship. . . . they add that it carries off those infirm weak bodies that would have been only a burden and a disgrace to their nation, and saves the victuals and clothing for better people that would have been expended on such useless creatures.

The flatness of the occiput seen among most Indians by white men penetrating the American wilderness gave rise to the popular fallacy that they all practiced artificial head deformation. Actually, in most instances, the flatness of the back of an Indian's head was the result of prolonged occipital contact with a resistant head support in the cradleboard. Except among a very few tribes, this type of deformation was unintentional.

Among some peoples in the South, along the Gulf of Mexico, on the north Pacific Coast, and west of the Cascade Mountains in the lower Columbia River Valley, intentional head deformation was a custom. It was achieved by pressure with boards or bindings against the soft cranial bones of an infant's head. Both the forehead and the back of the head might be deformed in this manner, with the parietals undergoing compensatory expansion. The most extreme deformation occurred among the Chinook, who regarded a low, slanting forehead and a flat occiput protruding above the top of the head as marks of beauty. The more grotesque the shape of the head—either a man's or woman's—the greater the social distinction its owner could claim.*

In the tribes of the Great Plains, the northern woodlands, the Northeast, the Southwest, and much of California, intentional head deformation is not known to have existed. The people erroneously called Flatheads, who dwelt in western Montana and Idaho, present an interesting case. Their proper name is Salish, which means simply "people." It was popularly thought for a long time by whites that they were given the name Flatheads by other Indians because they followed the practice of deforming the heads of infants. The opposite was true. They were designated as Flatheads because, unlike some of their congeners who lived farther to the west, they left their heads in a normal condition—that is, flat on top—instead of deforming them by pressure to slope toward the crown.

Head deformation was not a general custom in the Southeast, but it was practiced by the Wateree—now known to have belonged to the Siouan linguistic family—as evidenced by the account of Lawson, who was among this tribe shortly after 1700:

These Indians are of an extraordinary stature, and called by their neighbors flat heads, which seems a very suitable name for them.

* Mechanical head deformation was not, however, a custom peculiar to Indians. It was practiced among primitive peoples in Africa, Asia Minor, the South Pacific Islands, and some parts of Europe.

In their infancy, their nurses lay the back-part of their children's heads on a bag of sand (such as engravers use to rest their plates upon). They use a roll which is placed upon the babe's forehead, it being laid with its back upon a flat board, and swaddled hard down thereon, from one end of this engine to the other. This method makes the child's body and limbs as straight as an arrow. There being some young Indians that are perhaps crookedly inclined, at their first coming into the world, who are made perfectly straight by this method. I never saw an Indian of mature age that was any ways crooked, except by accident, and that way seldom; for they cure and prevent deformities of the limbs and body very exactly.

Lawson described the Wateree cradleboard as

a sort of a press, that is let out and in, more or less, according to the discretion of the nurse, in which they make the child's head flat; it makes the eyes stand a prodigious way asunder, and the hair hang over the forehead like the eves of a house, which seems very frightful. They being asked why they practiced this method, replied, the Indian's sight was much strengthened and quicker. . . .

It appears that head flattening, whether unintentional or otherwise, did little if any damage to a child. The famed anthropologist Hrdlicka, who made a careful study of the practice, is authority for the conclusion that

[the] effects of the various deformations on brain function and growth, as well as on the health of the individual, are apparently insignificant. The tribes that practice it show no indication of greater mortality at any age than those among which it does not exist, nor do they show a larger percentage of imbeciles, or of insane or neuropathic individuals. The deformation, once acquired, persists throughout life, the skull and brain compensating for the

compression by augmented extension in directions of least resistance.*

Mothers of all tribes—sometimes fathers—made dolls for their daughters. They were fashioned from stone, wood, clay, skin, corncobs, and even bread dough. Human hair was sometimes fastened to the head and dressed as the mother's, and a doll's clothing was representative of tribal style. Faces were painted, eyebrows were delineated, and tattoo marks were drawn on limbs. They were adorned with earrings, bracelets, and necklaces made of bone or shell. Women also made tiny cradleboards, tipis, and dishes—a little girl could care for her dolls and play house as she saw her mother doing in reality.

The small Hopi kachinas are famous throughout the world. It is improbable that any Indian doll is more beautifully and more elaborately costumed.

But among the Hopi, kachinas are not merely dolls or playthings. They are also living men dressed in kachina costumes that are symbolic representations, in human form, of the spirits of ancestors. The Hopi have about thirty chief male kachinas who take part in the most important annual ceremonies, but there are several hundred others who may appear at various times.

Kachina cults exist in each Hopi village. They might be likened to a number of Protestant churches in an American town of today, for, as Driver writes,

they shared much in common but at the same time had separate sets of officers and assembled in separate sacred structures . . . kivas.

* Hodge, 1906.

Boys are usually initiated into the Kachina Cults at ten or twelve years of age. Up to that time, they, along with the women and girls, are supposed to believe that the masked dancers are indeed supernatural visitors from the village of the spirits. . . . The boys are severely whipped by the kachina spirit-impersonating priests to impress them with the gravity of the occasion, to inspire awe of the supernatural, and to remove sickness and contamination from their persons. Then they are told that they are the ones who will wear the masked costumes in the future, thus making it clear that the dancers are human beings in disguise.

During the great spring ceremonies of the Hopi, the little kachinas are made by priests in the kivas. They are carefully fashioned of soft cottonwood, cotton cloth, feathers, and tiny strips of buckskin, with great attention given to the smallest details; they are ornamented with bits of shell, turquoise, and bone, and they may be masked or their faces may be painted and the features indicated.

These dolls are not worshipped. They are made expressly as presents for little girls, to whom they are presented on the morning of the last day of the festival by men who impersonate kachinas. In this way Hopi girls become thoroughly familiar with the complicated and symbolic masks, ornaments, and garments worn during tribal and religious ceremonials.

A medicine man of the Great Plains tribes might speak of four steep hills that marked the course of life on earth. While names for the hills varied according to languages and dialects, they all were connotative of infancy, youth, adulthood, and old age.

Consider the following scene: In a tipi standing in a cottonwood grove on the bank of the Platte River, long before any white man has crossed the sea of grass that reached to the sky on every side, a young mother of the Omaha tribe and a newborn child lie in a bed of soft skin robes. The admiring young father sits near them, fashioning a cradleboard with a flint knife. They have paid a medicine man to offer a prayer for the infant, and now he appears at the tipi entrance appropriately dressed and painted to perform the ceremony.

Francis La Flesche, an authority on Indian songs and ritual, provides this translation of one Omaha prayer that the shaman, with arms upheld in supplication, might have intoned to the gods of his people: *

> Ho! Ye Sun, Moon, Stars,
> All ye that move in the heavens,
> I bid ye hear me!
>
> Into your midst has come a new life.
> Consent ye, I implore!
> Make its path smooth, that it may
>   reach the brow of the first hill!
>
> Ho! Ye Winds, Clouds, Rain Mist,
> All ye that move in the air,
> I bid ye hear me!
>
> Into your midst has come a new life.
> Consent ye, I implore!
> Make its path smooth, that it may
>   reach the brow of the second hill!
>
> Ho! Ye Hills, Rivers, Valleys, Lakes,
>   Trees, Grasses,
> All ye of the earth,
> I bid ye hear me!

* See bibliography.

Into your midst has come a new life.
Consent ye, I implore!
Make its path smooth, that it may
   reach the brow of the third hill!

Ho! Ye Birds, great and small that
   fly in the air,
I bid ye hear me!
Into your midst has come a new life.

Ho! Ye Animals, great and small,
That dwell in the forest;
Ho! Ye Insects,
That creep among the grasses and
   burrow in the ground,
I bid ye hear me!

Into your midst has come a new life.
Consent ye, I implore!
Make its path smooth, that it may
   reach the brow of the fourth hill!

Ho!   All ye of the heavens, all ye of
   the air, all ye of the earth,
I bid ye hear me!

Into your midst has come a new life.
Consent ye, consent ye all, I implore!
Make its path smooth, then shall it
   travel beyond the four hills!

10
Health and Physique

The villages are free from nuisances, because they go outside to excrete, and they pass their water into clay vessels, which they empty at a distance from the village.

—Castaneda, describing Pueblo Indians, 1541

Aboriginal Indian women were both cleaner and healthier than white women of the American frontiers. This was true when the systematic destruction of western Indians began as it had been in colonial times.

Lawson noted about 1700 that Indian women of the Southeast were "hardier, sweeter, and had less travail" than either European women or white women of the American colonial settlements.

177

A few years later, John Brickell wrote of North Carolina Indians: *

they frequent the rivers in summertime very much where both men and women often go in naked to wash themselves, not both sexes together, yet this is not out of any point of modesty.

Vogel's excellent work on Indian medicine contains statements by several early observers showing that bathing was a universal practice among Indians. John D. Hunter † expressed the belief that the custom of bathing regularly which was followed by tribes west of the Mississippi

contributes very much to strengthen the body and invigorate the constitution. Men, women, and children, from early infancy, are in the daily habit of bathing, during the warm months, and not infrequently after cold weather has set in.

James Adair ‡ reported that Indians of the South bathed the year round, but that even in the cold northern woodlands this hygienic treatment was not neglected. Lewis H. Morgan,§ while traveling up the Missouri River, learned that northern Indians,

particularly those who sleep entirely nude, usually in the coldest weather, roll up their clothes in their blanket and go to the river and plunge in and wash themselves before they dress daily.

* *Natural History of North Carolina.*

† *Manners and Customs.*

‡ *History of American Indians.*

§ *Indian Journals.*

Father de Smet, the first religious to live among the Flatheads and other tribes of the north Pacific slope, stated that each morning "all wash themselves in a stream."

Indians living along the Pacific, Atlantic, and Gulf of Mexico coasts spent considerable time on the beaches and bathed regularly in salt water. Pueblos took their baths in the Rio Grande and its many affluents. Bathing was a ritual among the Yuman tribes of the hot desert country through which the Colorado River passed to the Gulf of California.

Many Americans erroneously think of the sweat bath as Scandinavian in origin. It came from Asia in two forms, both of which were diffused to various regions of the world. The two techniques are called "direct fire" and "water vapor," and primitive Indians used both, having brought them to North America across the Bering Strait thousands of years ago.

In the first method, sweating was induced by building a fire in a round, closed structure, some of which were very large, perhaps thirty to fifty feet in diameter, and constructed partially beneath ground level. It was used almost exclusively by men, for in many areas the large structures also served as men's clubs.

The water vapor method, used by both men and women, was a true steam bath. The sweathouses were small, sometimes only large enough to accommodate one person. Heated rocks were rolled into it, and water was poured over them. This type of sweatbath was by far the most widely used. Driver * states:

The water vapor technique is found all the way across Asia to Scandinavia and to Turkey, whence it diffused to North Africa

* *Op. cit.*

and Europe, where it is known as the Turkish bath. It was also employed in ancient Rome. Therefore, a single origin in northern Asia and subsequent diffusion to Europe on the west and to North America on the east seems likely.

Among most Indians sweat baths were not taken only for reasons of hygiene. They were used in the treatment of many illnesses; they also were social events; and in some tribes they were closely associated with religious ritual.

William H. Holmes * thinks that the religious motive "was by far the most important in the estimation of the Indians."

Holmes adds that, while sweating was important in medical practice,

the underlying idea was doubtless analogous to its religious and ceremonial use, since it was intended to influence disease spirits and was usually prescribed by the shaman, who sang outside and invoked the spirits while the patient was in the sweat-house. It was sometimes the friends and relatives of the sick person who, assembled in the sweat-house, sang and prayed for the patient's recovery.

Some sweathouses in which the water vapor method was used were large enough to accommodate several persons, perhaps as many as a score. A number of women might gather in one to chat and relax while enjoying the luxury of a steambath. Among tribes that made long hunting journeys, sweathouses might be constructed on the spur of the moment for a special purpose, but the sweathouses of sedentary peo-

* Hodge, 1906.

ples were also a communal ceremonial chamber. According to Driver: *

In the Southeast, the winter dwellings, called hothouses, are reminiscent of direct-fire sweathouses. Men, women, and children slept together in them with a fire going all night, arose together in the morning dripping with perspiration, and rushed out the door to the nearest stream for a cold bath.

Some tribes of the Northeast had large earth-covered sweathouses that were entered—like the kivas of the Pueblos—through a hole in the roof, and a crier might go through a village inviting everyone to join in a communal sweat bath. In most of California, sweathouses were permanent adjuncts of each village, and their use was always more or less associated with religious motives. It was the practice of some Pacific Coast groups to take daily sweat baths.

As a rule, a primitive Indian woman took pride in keeping her dwelling clean, as well as herself and members of her immediate family. Wrote Lawson:

I never felt any ill, unsavory smell in their cabins, whereas, should we live in our houses, as they do, we should be poisoned with our own nastiness, which confirms these Indians to be, as they really are, some of the sweetest people in the world.

Numerous Spanish adventurers spoke of the cleanliness of the Pueblos' houses, and this condition seemed to have changed little, if at all, when Hrdlicka observed them late in the last century. He wrote:

* *Op. cit.*

Except among the degraded, the old, or where the woman is indolent, the dwelling and its near surroundings are generally kept in fair good order and reasonably clean. During the day there is a freedom from bad odors in and about the dwelling. Some of the brush houses are pleasantly fragrant.*

For the tribes that moved frequently to hunt for game, to harvest natural foods in season, and to protect themselves from enemies—such as the people of the Great Plains, the Great Basin, the vast southwestern deserts, and the western mountains—sanitation was not a problem. Wherever they stopped, either for long or short periods, it was their custom to perform their bodily functions at a distance from their campgrounds. They were not unclean in this respect until Americans confined them in concentration camps, forcing them to endure unsanitary conditions which brought severe sickness and death to thousands of them.

Vogel † wrote:

Many tribes, especially in the far Southwest, followed the custom of incinerating everything connected with diseased persons, including their clothing, blankets, and lodges.

The Navajo carried such precautions to an extreme. While they did not burn a hogan in which a person had died, either from disease or from natural causes, they avoided it, and it stood empty until it crumbled into dust, for they believed that such a dwelling was inhabited by evil spirits.

The celebrated anthropologist Hrdlicka, always conserva-

* Hodge, 1906.

† *Op. cit.*

tive in his statements, expressed the opinion that the evidence available warranted "the conclusion that on the whole the Indian race was a comparatively healthy one." *

Yet he and other scientists readily admit there is a paucity of evidence to show what diseases prevailed among Indians north of Mexico before the advent of white people. There seems to be no doubt, however, that white men brought with them to the New World many of the terrible scourges that since time immemorial had swept through Europe.

Hrdlicka states that prehistoric Indians were not afflicted by

at least some of the epidemics and diseases of the Old World, such as smallpox and rachitis, while other scourges, such as tuberculosis, syphilis (pre-columbian), typhus, cholera, scarlet fever, cancer, etc., were rare, if occurring at all.

Father Louis Hennepin, a wilderness missionary for several years and a captive of the Sioux in Minnesota in 1680, wrote: †

Indians are very healthy. The men, the women, and even the children are extremely robust and consequently rarely sick. They do not know what it is to pamper themselves and accordingly are not subject to the thousand ailments that we incur by our too easy lives. Indians are not gouty, dropsical, or troubled with gravel or fever. They are always active and take so little rest that they are free from the ills that afflict most Europeans owing to lack of exercise. Almost never are they without appetite, even when they are

* Hodge, 1906.

† *Description of Louisiana.*

very old. Indians are usually so fond of eating that they get up at night to eat. . . . On the other hand, they endure very long fasts that no doubt would be unbearable to us. In case of necessity they go two or three days without eating and in spite of this carry on their hunting, fishing, or war without interruption.

Indian children are so hardened to cold that in mid-winter they run naked through the snow and wallow in it like little pigs without ill effect.

I admit that being constantly exposed to the open air helps in some ways to harden the Indians, but it must be that this extreme insensibility is due also to an unusually healthy constitution.

Women act as porters and are so strong that few European men can equal them. They carry loads that two or three of us could scarcely lift.

The women give birth to children without much labor.

Because the Southwest was the first region to be settled by Europeans, more is known of the health of the tribes residing there—such peoples as the Pueblos, the Yumans, the Navajo, the Pima, the Papago, and the Apache—than of that of Indians living elsewhere in the area of the United States. The chroniclers of the De Soto expedition say almost nothing about the matter—they were interested in finding gold, not in the well-being of Indians. Nunez Cabeza de Vaca wrote much on the subject, for he and his three companions were hailed as healers and obliged to minister to ailing persons in order to perform the roles expected of them, but their treatments were almost entirely psychological in nature. They knew nothing whatsoever of medicine, and his accounts of their practices contribute little to the history of curing maladies. Indeed, in almost every case, their patients cured themselves with the faith and confidence they placed in the powers of the strange visitors, whom they believed had descended from the sun.

There is evidence to support some reports that have come down to us through the centuries from early observers. Bones reveal a great deal to scientists. Other valuable sources are Indian traditions, and, as Hrdlicka notes, the existence among primitive Indians

of elaborate healing rites of ancient origin, their plant lore, in which curative properties are attributed to many vegetable substances, and the presence among them of a numerous class of professed healers, honored, feared, and usually well paid, would seem to indicate that diseases were not rare. . . .

If it may be safely asserted that they did not know such viral and communicable diseases as smallpox, scarlet fever, diphtheria, tuberculosis, and syphilis before the coming of white men, it may be said with equal confidence that they were not immune to arthritis, neuralgia, pleurisy, pneumonia, and various functional disorders. They suffered from ophthalmic conditions caused by smoke and sand, osteomyelitis and periostitis due to bone injury, and infection from wounds.

The statement often heard that Indian women aged early is without foundation. The condition was not general and was not characteristic of the race. When it occurred it was due entirely to conditions in the life of the individual. Neither wrinkling of the skin nor premature grayness occurred with greater incidence than among white women. The longevity of Indians, both men and women, was comparable to that of white persons. And just as in the white race, there were more aged Indian women than men. Diseases and functional disorders peculiar to women, including those of the puerperium, were much less common among Indians than among white women.

There were medicine women as well as medicine men among the tribes. No less than the men, the female healers were believed to be possessed of supernatural powers that enabled them to diagnose and cure afflictions. As the causes and the nature of diseases were mysteries, the Indian believed they were controlled by deities who had in some manner become offended. Thus, only by magic, ceremonies, and prayers, executed in a great variety of ways, could the angry spirit beings be appeased and the sickness cured.

There were also, however, medicine women who were thoroughly informed as to the efficacy and curative powers of certain medicines, who resorted only to tested practical methods of healing, and who made no claim to possession of supernatural powers. Faith in their treatment was all they asked of a patient. In reality, these knowledgeable women were herbalists, and many of them were midwives as well as healers.

The extent of the knowledge of medicines possessed by prehistoric Indians may be judged from the following statement by Vogel:

170 drugs which have been or still are official in the *Pharmacopeia of the United States of America* or the *National Formulary* were used by North American Indians north of Mexico, and about fifty more were used by Indians of the West Indies, Mexico, and Central and South America. Hundreds more which have not become official drugs were used. . . .

While the aboriginal uses of these drugs were frequently incorrect in the judgment of modern science, the examples of efficacious usage which have been cited constitute an imposing monument to the original Americans. There can be no doubt that by trial-and-error methods they arrived at an understanding of the properties and effects of many useful botanical medicines.

It seems evident that at the time of the first conquests by white men in the region of the United States, Indians were perhaps somewhat healthier than their ancestors who had preceded them by several thousand years. Archeologist John Witthoft prepared this description of the Archaic Age Indians who dwelt in the northeastern forests, perhaps as early as 6000 B.C.: *

a small man, rarely more than five feet, five inches tall. He was of very slight build and probably weighed no more than 130 pounds. His bones were especially light and delicate as compared with almost all other human types. Delicate modeling of the facial bones and thinness of the skull bones is conspicuous in Indian skeletons. Despite this, he was almost always an exceedingly muscular man, as is indicated by the form of those parts of his bones which were at the ends of muscle bundles.

All evidence from the skeletons suggests that the Indian was wiry, strong and extremely tough. He had a strongly sculptured face as compared to the Caucasian, with jutting cheek bones and a large, well-developed palate and dental arch. Despite this, his teeth were subject to the same decay and diseases as ours, and to much more wear; he had ordinarily lost all but a few of them before he was thirty-five years old. He did not chew the way we do, but bit his tough food with his incisors edge-to-edge, grinding with his front teeth and molars.

The Indian of the forest seldom lived to his fortieth birthday, usually dying before he was thirty-five. His diseased teeth and the infections they caused were probably a prelude to death. Hunger, exposure, and hunting accidents were probably the other major causes of early death. Various arthritic and rheumatoid diseases were remarkably frequent and often severe, judging by evidence from the skeletons.

* *Indian Prehistory in Pennsylvania.*

Indian women differed as greatly as white women in physique and anatomical characteristics. While their hair color was predominantly a somewhat lustrous black, there were many whose hair contained slight brownish and bluish tinges. Their skin color ranged from bronze through many shades of brown to a dark coppery tint, and in some tribes skin color approached chocolate and other dark shades. The color of their eyes varied from coal to hazel and dark brown, and the iris was often surrounded with a narrow but clearly marked ring.

In some Pacific Coast and Pueblo tribes, women were usually of very short stature, seldom standing more than five feet in height. In other California and Pueblo tribes, and among the Apache, Navajo, Comanche, Ute, Paiute, Shoshoni, Kiowa, Cherokee, and Chickasaw, they were somewhat taller, perhaps averaging five feet five inches in height. Indian women of greater height were found among the Yuma, Mohave, Pima, Nez Perce, Sioux, Crow, Cheyenne, Arapaho, Iroquois, Chippewa, and Algonquian tribes. However, rarely was an Indian woman more than six feet tall.

Indians came from many regions of the Old World. Thus, their physical characteristics presented wide variances. People of different bloods had moved through the land mass of Asia long before any peoples moved into the land mass of the Western Hemisphere. Perhaps not very many had moved into Asia proper from Africa and the eastern Mediterranean—that cannot be said—but even a few would have been enough to leave telltale marks of their different bloods. And the peoples who moved on to North America across the Bering Strait land bridge, or even after the connection between the two continents had become shallow water interspersed with islands, would bear those telltale marks. Still, they would be minimal, and Mongoloid features would be dominant. Hrdlicka states that while Indians

show many minor and even some important physical variations, and can be separated into several physical types, they present throughout the continent so many features in common that they properly may be regarded as one great race, admitting of a general anatomical description.*

One of the notable physical variations is cranial structure. The three principal classes of cranial form are represented among Indians north of Mexico. For example: women of the Algonquian, most Siouan and Great Plains tribes, the Shoshoni, the Taos, and the Pima had long heads. Among Indian groups in Florida, among the Mound Builders of the Midwest and the ancient Pueblos, and among the Apache, Walapai, Havasupai, Nez Perce, Hopi, Zuni, Navajo, Yuman, Comanche, and Winnebago, women were short-headed or broad-headed. Heads types of more moderate proportions, which could not be included in either the long or broad classifications, were predominate in numerous widely separated peoples, such as California tribes, some Siouans, the Cherokee of the South, and the Iroquois of the Northeast. It is clearly apparent, therefore, that Asiatic peoples distinguished by cranial variations became established in close proximity to each other in both ancient and late prehistoric periods.

Driver sums up information on the subject in these words: †

* *Op. cit.*

† *Indians of North America.*

The physical type of the Paleo-Indian shows some differences from that of contemporary Indians, who are classed as Mongoloids by all anthropologists. . . . On the whole the earliest Indians had longer and narrower skulls, with heavier jaws and teeth. Muscle attachments on the bones of the limbs as well as on the skull were heavier, indicating a more heavily muscled individual. The longitudinal crests of some of these early skulls tend to form a sort of ridge, with the skull bones sloping away somewhat like the two-pitched roof of a house from the ridge pole. This is a primitive characteristic found in pre-*sapiens* species of fossil men.

However, all bones of Paleo-Indians so far discovered are unquestionably *Homo sapiens*, and some individuals fail to exhibit any of the primitive features and could even pass for contemporary Indians. On the whole, however, the Paleo-Indian is less Mongoloid than contemporary Indians, although the latter show variation in this respect.

It therefore appears that the first immigrants to America from northeast Asia date from a time when the European (Caucasoid) and Asiatic (Mongoloid) races were less differentiated than at the present time. The Paleo-Indian belongs to a more generalized type of Caucasoid-Mongoloid race with a slight bias in favor of the Mongoloid. As time went by and the Mongoloid race became more and more dominant in northeast Asia, successive waves of immigrants [to North America] became more and more Mongoloid.

Martin, Quimby, and Collier add: *

it is impossible to characterize an "Indian" in any brief, general manner. The Indian as we know him today is not pure Mongoloid or pure anything else. . . . The successive waves of Asiatic migrants represented a composite of several racial strains, some bearing Mediterranean strains, some bearing Oceanic Negroid strains, and most of them bearing Mongoloid strains . . . the primary

* *Indians Before Columbus.*

divergencies of physical types, now observable in the American Indians, first appeared in Asia and then were perpetuated in the New World.

The noted anthropologist Earnest A. Hooten is credited with the observation that when people of different races meet they *usually* fight but they *always* interbreed.

In the eyes of European men—standards of judgment being what they were—few Indian women were beautiful. Indeed, the word *beauty* rarely appears in old documents with reference to their faces. There are in the accounts of early explorers and travelers, however, no end of statements unreservedly expounding on the shapeliness of their limbs and breasts and other bodily charms—obviously anatomical features white men found no less admirable than those of the girls left behind them across the sea. Enthusiasm marked many of the encomiums, as illustrated in Lawson's tribute of 1701 to the Indian women of Carolina:

when young, and at maturity, they are as fine shaped creatures, (take them generally), as any in the universe. They are of a tawny complexion, their eyes very brisk and amorous, their smiles afford the finest composure a face can possess, their hands are of the finest make, with small, long fingers, and as soft as their cheeks, and their whole bodies of a smooth nature. They are not so uncouth or unlikely as we suppose them, nor are they any strangers or not proficients of the soft passion.

Dating very old bones is difficult and dangerous, and scientists, understandably, are extremely cautious and always hesitant to voice firm conclusions. They have, as Ceram states,*

* *The First American.*

learned caution from a great many disconcerting experiences. They no longer regard a single dating as sufficient. They insist on double and triple proofs, and lay special weight on the oldest method of proof in their profession: stratigraphy.

It is interesting to note, however, that the oldest bones found in the United States to which dates can be ascribed with a certain degree of scientific accuracy are skeletal remains of women. The finds were made in Minnesota, California, and Texas, and while the ages given to them by some anthropologists are far from being acceptable to many other scientists, they nevertheless remain in the forefront of the United States *Homo sapiens* antiquity derby—a never-ending race—at the moment of this writing.

An ornament Miss Minnesota had worn was found first. It had tumbled out of a road being excavated through a gravel deposit, some ten feet below ground surface, in 1930. A grader operator, attracted by the shiny white object, climbed off his machine and picked it up. It appeared to be part of a shell. Then he saw that nearby some bones were exposed.

Their curiosity stirred, the highway workers paused in their duties to do a little digging by hand. They soon came upon a human skull and part of a skeleton. As they removed these remains, they found among them a knife about nine inches in length which had been made from an elk antler, and a conch shell with two perforations. The conch shell lay among the ribs and vertebrae of the abdominal area.

Word of the discovery, which was made near Pelican Rapids in western Minnesota, was sent to the University of Minnesota, and archeologist A. E. Jenks hurried to the scene. He felt like crying when he saw the damage that had been done, for he realized at once that a find of transcending importance had been made.

While the workmen had handled the skull with care, their removing it from the gravel had prevented trained observers from viewing it in situ. Jenks and several aides, however, began a careful excavation of the site, and they recovered in situ other bone fragments, some of which could be fitted to those found by the road builders.

It was not so much the finding of the bones as the location in which they had been found that caused excitement in the scientific world. The gravel through which the cut was being made was the bed of an ancient lake, known as Glacial Lake Pelican, which had formed shortly after the retreat of the last continental ice sheet, perhaps some twenty thousand years ago, and several millennia later had become extinct.

Miss Minnesota was probably about fifteen years old when she met death. If beauty contests were held in the Pleistocene—and who can say they were not?—she would not have won even a consolation prize. As Jenks described her, among the most important primitive morphological characteristics of her skull "was the lack of reduction of the jaw and teeth." *

The eminent archeologist H. M. Wormington † noted that

[her] teeth are, in fact, extraordinarily large, even larger than those of certain Paleolithic men. The cusp pattern of the molars is of a primitive type. The upper incisors are shovel-shaped, a trait ordinarily associated with Mongoloids. There is a marked protrusion of the portions of the upper and lower jaws which contain the front teeth and a pronounced backward extension of the skull which is narrow relative to its length.

* *Pleistocene Man in Minnesota.*

† *Ancient Man in North America.*

To most scientists, however, Miss Minnesota is utterly beautiful. She is also the object of a controversy that has continued for more than forty years, and may never be settled. Nevertheless, certain factors in the case are beyond dispute. The perforated shell found in her rib cage, which she probably wore as a pendant on a thong, has been identified as a marine shell of a species found on the Gulf of Mexico. Obviously, since she had it in her possession, there must have been contact between Paleo-Indians of Minnesota and people living farther south. The most reasonable assumption is that the ornament reached Minnesota through trade channels.

The depth at which Miss Minnesota was found strongly supports the contention of anthropologists and geologists that she lived in the Pleistocene. It seems illogical to think that she would have been interred in a grave ten feet deep. The suggestion that she might have been buried in a landslide is not substantiated by the geology of the site. Even if she had fallen or had been buried in an open pit ten feet deep, it would be necessary to assume, as some archeologists point out, that the crack had been closed over again without crushing or disturbing the bones, a most unlikely occurrence. And even if that had happened, the girl's skeleton still would belong to the Pleistocene, for, according to Wormington, the special climatic and topographical conditions * necessary to induce landsliding "would be associated with a period almost as remote as the varve formation in which her bones were found."

And that varve clay formation, geologists state, belonged to the Pleistocene and was laid down some eleven thousand years ago. But that is not sufficient proof for some scientists

* *Op. cit.*

that Miss Minnesota's bones are eleven thousand years old—not by a long shot.

Laguna Girl traveled much farther as a skull than she did during her lifetime. What was left of her was found in 1933 by two youths digging for treasure in Laguna Beach, California. The skull received a blow from a pickaxe while it was being excavated from hard earth, but fortunately was not seriously damaged. Howard Wilson, one of the treasure hunters, took the skull home. His mother advised him to throw it in the garbage can, but he disobeyed her and stowed it in a box. During the next four years it was examined by scientists at several Southern California museums, and all of them agreed that, while it was interesting, it was not of unusual age. Wilson returned the skull to its box in disappointment.

There it remained for sixteen years!

Meanwhile Wilson was busy pursuing a career as a designer, but he had not lost interest in archeology. Nor had he ceased to believe that the skull was older than the anthropologists who had examined it had estimated. In 1953 he sent it to a sculptor, George Stromer, who specialized in making sculptures of prehistoric men. Stromer was intrigued and showed it to J. J. Markey, an anthropologist, who found it interesting enough to seek other opinions.

Markey took the skull with him to Paris, London, Madrid, Rome, and Brussels. Leading anthropologists in all those capitals studied it, but, as Ceram notes, the judgments they handed down were "anything but definitive."

For eight years Laguna Girl traveled from museum to museum, university to university, and then was sent back home to Wilson. He put her back in the box, where she remained until 1967.

In that year, still believing that the skull was unusual and of great anthropological value, Wilson managed to gain an audience with the famous L. S. B. Leakey, who was in California on a lecture tour. After only a few minutes' study of the skull, Leakey decided that it should be sent to Rainer Berger at the University of California.

Berger and other scientists used the most modern techniques, including the radio carbon (C-14) dating method, in their examinations of Laguna Girl's cranium. Their findings electrified scientists throughout the world.

The skull was between 18,260 and 15,680 years old!

Said Berger in his report: "It is thus the oldest direct evidence of Man in the Americas."

Perhaps he is correct, and undoubtedly the findings he reported about Laguna Girl are accurate. Still, there are other scientists who are inclined to believe that another contestant is leading the race. She is Midland Minnie of Texas.

The first part of Midland Minnie was found in a sand blowout near the western Texas town for which she has been named. She was not all together. Fortunately for science, her discoverer was a competent amateur archeologist, Keith Glasscock, from Pampa, Texas. He had been examining the desolate area and had discovered several ancient artifacts. The wind was blowing wildly on the June day in 1953 when he came upon some human bone fragments in the bottom of a sand blowout. They were highly mineralized. Glasscock sensed at once that he had made a major find, which, indeed, was true.

Looking about he found other skeletal remains, parts of a human skull, a first rib, and two metacarpals. These, which he did not disturb, were, according to anthropologist Fred

Wendorf, "in process of being exposed by wind cutting into a grayish sand in the floor of the blowout." *

Glasscock picked up some fragments, including parts of the skull, that were in danger of being blown away and shattered, and hurried back to Midland, realizing the necessity of enlisting the aid of specialists. He mailed the bone fragments to Wendorf, then at the Laboratory of Anthropology in Santa Fe. When Wendorf noted the degree of fossilization and the presence of a thick, calcerous accretion on the skull, he promptly got in touch with the distinguished scientist Alex Krieger. Accompanied by several prominent archeologists, they went to the site and began work.

For the first time in the United States, human bones, besides the skull of Midland Minnie, were found in unquestionable association with extinct Pleistocene faunal remains.

Midland Minnie was probably thirty years of age at the time of death. To T. D. Stewart, curator of physical anthropology at the Smithsonian Institution, fell the difficult task of putting her long-shattered head together. He was able to assemble a large portion of the skull, containing about sixty pieces. Stewart had some of Midland Minnie's teeth, but her lower jaw was missing. All the recovered teeth belonged to the upper jaw. An abnormally placed tooth was located in the floor of the nasal cavity. Clearly Midland Minnie had been in need of a dentist.

Tests by several methods of extinct animal bones, Midland Minnie's remains, and other objects recovered at the site produced various dates. Carbon extracted from caliche stones used in cooking fires yielded a date in excess of twenty thousand years. The Rosholt "uranium clock" technique gave fos-

* *Midland Discovery.*

sils from Midland Minnie's resting place and nearby blow-outs ages ranging from nineteen thousand to fifteen thousand years.

Wendorf wrote:

In its hardness, degree of mineralization, and chemical proper-ties, the human being [that is, Midland Minnie] is just as much a Pleistocene fossil as any of the extinct vertebrates discovered at this site.

And he added the significant statement:

The present age determinations are *ceiling dates.* That is, the true dates cannot be younger, *but they can be older.*

Midland Minnie undoubtedly is older than Miss Min-nesota, but whether she is older than Laguna Girl remains a matter of controversy among scientists.

However, Midland Minnie stands alone in one scientific category. Her windblown bones are older than any other human remains found in the United States in unmistakable association with the bones of mammals that lived long before the last of the great glaciers of the Ice Age had vanished from North America—an honor that would stir envy in any self-respecting, ambitious Pleistocene girl.

Selected Bibliography

ADAIR, JAMES. *The History of the American Indians: Particularly Those Nations Adjoining to the Mississippi.* London, 1775.

AMSDEN, CHARLES AVERY. *Prehistoric Southwesterners from Basketmaker to Pueblo.* Los Angeles: Southwest Museum, 1949.

BAHTI, TOM. *Southwestern Indian Tribes.* Flagstaff, Ariz., 1968.

————. *Southwestern Indian Arts and Crafts.* Flagstaff, 1970.

————. *Southwestern Indian Ceremonials.* Flagstaff, 1971.

BANCROFT, HUBERT HOWE. *Native Races.* 5 vols. San Francisco, 1886–1890.

BARTRAM, WILLIAM. *Travels in the Southern Regions of the United States.* Philadelphia, 1791.

————. *Observations on the Creek and Cherokee Indians.* New York: American Philosophical Society, 1853.

BENAVIDES, ALONSO DE. *Memorial of 1630.* Trans. Mrs. Edward E. Ayers. Chicago, 1916; Albuquerque, 1965.

BERGER, RAINER, and JAMES R. SACKETT. *Final Report on the Laguna Beach Excavation of the Isotope Foundation.* Berkeley, 1969.

BOAS, FRANZ. *Chinook Texts.* Bureau of American Ethnology, Bulletin 20. Washington, 1894.

Selected Bibliography

BOLTON, HERBERT EUGENE. *Spanish Exploration in the Southwest.* New York, 1916.

———. *The Spanish Borderlands.* New Haven, 1921.

———. *Coronado.* New York, 1949.

BRICKELL, JOHN. *The Natural History of North Carolina.* Dublin, 1737; Raleigh, 1911.

CASTANEDA, PEDRO DE. *Narrative of the Expedition of Coronado.* Trans. George Parker Winship. Bureau of American Ethnology, 14th Report. Washington, 1896.

CERAM, C. W. *The First American.* New York, 1971.

CHITTENDEN, HIRAM MARTIN, and ALBERT TALBOT RICHARDSON. *The Life, Letters and Travels of Father Pierre-Jean de Smet.* New York, 1905.

COON, CARLETON S. *The Story of Man.* New York, 1962.

CORKRAN, DAVID H. *The Creek Frontier, 1540–1783.* Norman, Okla., 1967.

CULIN, STEWART. *American Indian Games.* Bureau of American Ethnology, 24th Report. Washington, 1905.

CUMMINGS, BYRON. *Kinishba.* Tucson, Ariz., 1940.

CURTIN, L. S. M. *Preparation of Sacred Corn Meal in the Rio Grande Pueblos.* Los Angeles: Southwest Museum, 1968.

CUSHING, FRANK HAMILTON. *Zuni Fetishes.* Bureau of American Ethnology, 2nd Report. Washington, 1883.

———. *Outlines of Zuni Creation Myths.* Bureau of American Ethnology, 13th Report. Washington, 1896.

———. *A Study of Pueblo Pottery as Illustrative of Zuni Culture Growth.* Bureau of American Ethnology, 4th Report. Washington, 1886.

DEBO, ANGIE. *The Rise and Fall of the Choctaw Republic.* Norman, Okla., 1934.

DE SMET, PIERRE-JEAN (See Chittenden; Terrell, 1963).

DORSEY, J. OWEN. *Omaha Sociology.* Bureau of American Ethnology, 3rd Report. Washington, 1884.

———. *Osage Traditions.* Bureau of American Ethnology, 6th Report. Washington, 1888.

———. *A Study of Siouan Cults.* Bureau of American Ethnology, 11th Report. Washington, 1894.

———. *Omaha Dwellings, Furniture and Implements.* Bureau of American Ethnology, 13th Report. Washington, 1896.

DOZIER, EDWARD P. *The Pueblo Indians of North America.* New York, 1970.

DRIVER, HAROLD E. *Indians of North America.* Chicago, 1961.

DRUCKER, PHILIP. *Indians of the Northwest Coast.* New York, 1955.

EGGAN, FRED. *Social Organization of the Western Pueblos.* Chicago, 1950.

ENGELMANN, GEORGE J. *Labor Among Primitive Peoples.* St. Louis, 1884.

EWERS, JOHN C. *Indian Life on the Upper Missouri.* Norman, Okla., 1968.

FERGUSON, ERNA. *Dancing Gods.* Albuquerque, N.Mex., 1931.

FEWKES, J. WALTER. *Tusayan Katcinas.* Bureau of American Ethnology, 15th Report. Washington, 1897.

———. *Antiquities of Mesa Verde National Park: Cliff Palace.* Bureau of American Ethnology. Washington, 1911.

———. *Ancestor Worship of the Hopi Indians.* Washington: Smithsonian Institution, 1921.

FIELD, CLARK. *The Art and Romance of Indian Basketry.* Tulsa, Okla., 1964.

FLETCHER, ALICE C. *The Hako, a Pawnee Ceremony.* Bureau of American Ethnology, 22nd Report. Washington, 1903.

GATSCHET, ALBERT SAMUEL. *The Klamath Indians.* Bureau of American Ethnology. Washington, 1890.

GIBBS, GEORGE. *Tribes of Western Washington and Northwestern Oregon.* Bureau of American Ethnology. Washington, 1890.

GLADWIN, HAROLD S., E. W. HAURY, E. B. SAYLES, and NORA GLADWIN. *Excavation of Snaketown: Material Culture.* Globe, Ariz., 1937.

GOODWIN, GRENVILLE. *The Social Organization of the Western Apache.* Tucson, Ariz., 1942.

GOOKIN, DANIEL. *Historical Collections of the Indians of New England.* Boston: Massachusetts Historical Society, 1792.

HASSRICK, ROYAL B. *The Sioux: Life and Customs of a Warrior Society.* Norman, Okla., 1964.

HENNEPIN, LOUIS. *Description of Louisiana.* Paris, 1683; Minneapolis, 1938.

HEWITT, J. N. B. "Orenda." In Frederick W. Hodge (Ed.), *Hankbook of American Indians North of Mexico.* Bureau of American Ethnology, Bulletin 30. Washington, 1906. Vol. 2.

HIBBEN, FRANK C. "Was Ice Age Man a Game Hog?" *Denver Post,* August 10, 1969.

HODGE, FREDERICK W. (Ed.). *Handbook of American Indians North of Mexico.* 2 vols. Bureau of American Ethnology, Bulletin 30. Washington, 1906.

HODGE, FREDERICK W. and THEODOR W. LEWIS (Eds.). *Spanish Explorers in the Southern United States*. New York, 1907. (Contains narratives of Cabeza de Vaca, De Soto, and Coronado expeditions.)

HOFFMAN, WALTER J. *The Menomini Indians*. Bureau of American Ethnology, 14th Report. Washington, 1896.

HOLMES, WILLIAM H. *Art in Shell of the Ancient Americans*. Bureau of American Ethnology, 2nd Report. Washington, 1883.

————. *Prehistoric Textile Fabrics of the United States Derived from Impressions on Pottery*. Bureau of American Ethnology, 3rd Report. Washington, 1884.

————. *Pottery of the Ancient Pueblos*. Bureau of American Ethnology, 4th Report. Washington, 1886.

————. *Ancient Pottery of the Mississippi Valley*. Bureau of American Ethnology, 4th Report. Washington, 1886.

————. *Prehistoric Textile Art of the Eastern United States*. Bureau of American Ethnology, 13th Report. Washington, 1896.

————. "Sweating." In Frederick W. Hodge (Ed.), *Handbook of American Indians North of Mexico*. Bureau of American Ethnology, Bulletin 30. Washington, 1906. Vol. 1.

————. "Sweat-houses." In Frederick W. Hodge (Ed.), *Handbook of American Indians North of Mexico*. Bureau of American Ethnology, Bulletin 30, Washington, 1906. Vol. 2.

HOOTEN, E. A. *Indians of Pecos Pueblo*. New Haven: Philips Academy, 1930.

HORGAN, PAUL. *Great River: The Rio Grande in North American History*. New York, 1954.

HOUGH, WALTER. "Dyes and Pigments." In Frederick W. Hodge (Ed.), *Handbook of American Indians North of Mexico*. Bureau of American Ethnology, Bulletin 30. Washington, 1906. Vol. 1.

HRDLICKA, ALES. "Physiology." In Frederick W. Hodge (Ed.), *Handbook of American Indians North of Mexico*. Bureau of American Ethnology, Bulletin 30. Washington, 1906. Vol. 2.

————. *Physiological and Medical Observations Among the Indians of Southwestern United States and Northern Mexico*. Bureau of American Ethnology. Washington, 1908.

HUNTER, JOHN D., *Manners and Customs of Several Indian Tribes Located West of the Mississippi*. Philadelphia, 1823; Minneapolis, 1957.

JENKS, ALBERT ERNEST. *Prehistoric Man in Minnesota*. Minneapolis, 1936.

JONES, WILLIAM. *Ethnography of the Fox Indians.* Bureau of American Ethnology. Washington, 1939.

JOSEPHY, ALVIN M. *The Indian Heritage of America.* New York, 1968.

JOSSELYN, JOHN. *An Account of Two Voyages to New England Made During the Years 1638, 1663.* Boston, 1865.

KIRK, DONALD R. *Wild Edible Plants of the Western United States.* Healdsburg, Calif., 1970.

KLUCKHOHN, CLYDE, and DOROTHEA LEIGHTON. *The Navajo.* Cambridge, Mass., 1946.

KROEBER, A. L. *Handbook of the Indians of California.* Bureau of American Ethnology. Washington, 1925; Berkeley, 1953.

LA FLESCHE, FRANCIS. "Omaha Prayer." *Journal of American Folklore,* 1905.

———. *The Osage Tribe: Rite of the Chiefs: Sayings of the Ancient Men.* Bureau of American Ethnology. Washington, 1921.

LANGE, CHARLES H. *Cochiti, a New Mexico Pueblo.* Carbondale, Ill., 1959.

LATTA, F. F. *Handbook of Yokuts Indians.* Oildale, Calif., 1949.

LAWSON, JOHN. *History of North Carolina.* London, 1714; Richmond, Va., 1937.

LEWIS, MERIWETHER, and WILLIAM CLARK. *The Lewis and Clark Expedition.* Philadelphia, 1814.

LOWIE, ROBERT H. *Primitive Society.* New York, 1947.

———. *Indians of the Plains.* New York, 1954.

LUMMIS, CHARLES F. "Fray Zarate Salmeron's Relation." *Land of Sunshine Magazine,* Vols. 11 and 12, 1897–1898.

MACCAULEY, CLAY. *The Seminole Indians of Florida.* Bureau of American Ethnology, 5th Report. Washington, 1887.

MATTHEWS, JOHN JOSEPH. *The Osages: Children of the Middle Waters.* Norman, Oklahoma, 1961.

McGEE, W. J. *The Sioux Indians.* Bureau of American Ethnology, 15th Report. Washington, 1897.

McHUGH, TOM. *The Time of the Buffalo.* New York, 1972.

MANGELSDORF, P. C., and C. EARLE SMITH, JR. *New Archeological Evidence on Evolution in Maize.* Cambridge, Mass., 1949.

MARTIN, PAUL S., GEORGE I. QUIMBY, and DONALD COLLIER. *Indians Before Columbus.* Chicago, 1947.

Selected Bibliography

MASON, OTIS T. "Basketry." In Frederick W. Hodge (Ed.), *Handbook of American Indians North of Mexico*. Bureau of American Ethnology, Bulletin 30. Washington, 1906.

MATTHEWS, WASHINGTON. *The Mountain Chant: A Navajo Ceremony*. Bureau of American Ethnology, 5th Report. Washington, 1887.

MERA, H. P. *The Rain Bird: A Study in Pueblo Design*. Santa Fe: Laboratory of Anthropology, 1937.

MERENESS, NEWTON D. *Travels in the American Colonies*. New York, 1916.

MOONEY, JAMES. *The Sacred Formulas of the Cherokee*. Bureau of American Ethnology, 7th Report. Washington, 1891.

———. *The Siouan Tribes of the East*. Bureau of American Ethnology, Bulletin 22. Washington, 1894.

———. *Myths of the Cherokee*. Bureau of American Ethnology, 19th Report. Washington, 1900.

———. "Skin Dressing." In Frederick W. Hodge (Ed.), *Handbook of American Indians North of Mexico*. Bureau of American Ethnology, Bulletin 30. Washington, 1906. Vol. 2.

MORGAN, LEWIS H. *Houses and House-Life of the American Aborigines*. Bureau of American Ethnology. Washington, 1881.

———. *Indian Journals, 1859–1862*. Ann Arbor, Mich., 1959.

NEWCOMB, W. W., JR. *The Indians of Texas*. Austin, Tex., 1961.

NUNEZ CABEZA DE VACA, ALVAR. *Relacion*. Zamora, Spain, 1542.

ORTIZ, ALFONSO. *The Tewa World*. Chicago, 1969.

PARSONS, ELSIE CLEWS. *Isleta, New Mexico*. Bureau of American Ethnology, 47th Report. Washington, 1929.

———. *Pueblo Indian Religion*. 2 vols. Chicago, 1939.

PAYNE, JOHN HOWARD. *Cherokee Manuscripts* (in Newberry Library, Chicago.)

PEPPER, G. H. *Pueblo Bonito*. New York: American Museum of Natural History, 1920.

POLLARD, J. G. *The Pamunkey Indians of Virginia*. Bureau of American Ethnology, Bulletin 17. Washington, 1894.

POWELL, JOHN WESLEY. *Indian Linguistic Families of America North of Mexico*. Bureau of American Ethnology, 7th Report. Washington, 1891.

————. *Sketch of the Mythology of the North American Indians*. Bureau of American Ethnology, 1st Report. Washington, 1881.

POWERS, STEPHEN. *Tribes of California*. Bureau of American Ethnology. Washington, 1877.

QUEBBEMAN, FRANCES E. *Medicine in Territorial Arizona*. Phoenix, Ariz. 1966.

SAYLES, E. B., and ERNEST ANTEVS. *The Cochise Culture*. Globe, Ariz., 1941.

SCHOOLCRAFT, HENRY R. *Personal Memoirs of a Residence of Thirty Years with the Indian Tribes on the American Frontier, A.D. 1812–1842*. Philadelphia, 1851.

SKINNER, ALANSON. *Observations on the Ethnology of the Sauk Indians*. Milwaukee, 1924.

SMITH, BUCKINGHAM. *Relacion of Alvar Nunez Cabeza de Vaca*. Translated from the 1555 edition. Washington 1851.

SMITH, ERMINNIE A. *Myths of the Iroquois*. Bureau of American Ethnology, 2nd Report. Washington, 1883.

STERLING, M. W. *Original Myth of Acoma and Other Records*. Bureau of American Ethnology. Washington, 1942.

STEVENSON, MATILDA C. *The Religious Life of the Zuni Child*. Bureau of American Ethnology, 5th Report. Washington, 1887.

————. *The Sia*. Bureau of American Ethnology, 11th Report. Washington, 1894.

————. *The Zuni Indians*. Bureau of American Ethnology. Washington, 1904.

SWANTON, JOHN R. "Puberty." In Frederick W. Hodge (Ed.), *Handbook of American Indians North of Mexico*. Bureau of American Ethnology, Bulletin 30. Washington, 1906.

————. *Indian Tribes of North America*. Bureau of American Ethnology. Washington, 1952.

TERRELL, JOHN UPTON. *Journey into Darkness*. New York, 1962.

————. *Black Robe*. New York, 1964.

————. *Traders of the Western Morning*. Los Angeles: Southwest Museum, 1967.

————. *La Salle: The Life and Times of an Explorer*. New York, 1968.

————. *Estevanico the Black.* Los Angeles, 1968.

————. *The Navajos.* New York, 1970.

————. *American Indian Almanac.* New York, 1971.

————. *Apache Chronicle.* New York, 1972.

————. *Pueblos, Gods, and Spaniards.* New York, 1973.

THOMAS, CYRUS. *Burial Mounds in the Northern Sections of the United States.* Bureau of American Ethnology, 5th Report. Washington, 1887.

————. *Report of Mound Explorations.* Bureau of American Ethnology, 12th Report. Washington, 1894.

THWAITES, RUEBEN GOLD (Ed.). *Jesuit Relations and Allied Documents, 1610–1791.* 73 vols. Cleveland, Ohio, 1896–1901.

UNDERHILL, RUTH. *The Red Man's Religion.* Chicago, 1965.

VAN DER DONCK, A. *A Description of New Netherlands.* New York: New York Historical Society, 1841.

VILLAGRA, GASPAR PEREZ DE. *History of New Mexico.* Trans. Gilbert Espinosa. Los Angeles, 1933.

VOGEL, VIRGIL J. *American Indian Medicine.* Norman, Okla., 1970.

WALLACE, ERNEST, and E. ADAMSON HOEBEL. *The Comanches, Lords of the South Plains.* Norman, Okla., 1952.

WATKINS, FRANCES E. *Hopi Toys.* Los Angeles: Southwest Museum, n.d.

WEDEL, WALDO R. *Prehistoric Man on the Great Plains.* Norman, Okla., 1961.

WENDORF, FRED, ALEX D. KRIEGER, CLAUDE C. ALBRITTON, and T. D. STEWART. *The Midland Discovery.* Austin, Tex., 1955.

WHITE, LESLIE A. *The Acoma Indians.* Bureau of American Ethnology. Washington, 1932.

————. *Pueblo of Santo Domingo.* Menasha, Wisc.: American Anthropological Association, 1942.

WHITING, ALFRED F. *Ethnobotany of the Hopi.* Flagstaff, Ariz., 1966.

WINSHIP, GEORGE PARKER (Trans.). *The Narrative of the Expedition of Coronado by Castaneda.* Bureau of American Ethnology, 14th Report. Washington, 1896.

WITTHOFT, JOHN. *Indian Prehistory of Pennsylvania.* Harrisburg, Pa., 1965.

WOODWARD, GRACE STEELE. *The Cherokees.* Norman, Okla., 1963.

Wormington, H. M. *Prehistoric Indians of the Southwest.* Denver: Denver Museum of Natural History, 1947.

———. *Ancient Man in North America.* Denver: Denver Museum of Natural History, 1957.

Wormington, H. M., and Arminta Neal. *The Story of Pueblo Pottery.* Denver: Denver Museum of Natural History, 1951.

Index